GPS
God's Plan for Significance

A Road Map for the Rest of Your Life

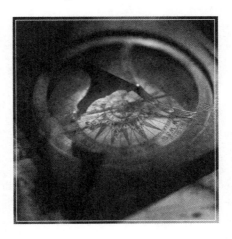

Jerry and Shirley Rose
SigLiv Publishing

ISBN: 0-9770642-3-9
                               9-780977-064236

Publisher: SigLiv Publishing/Total Living Network

Editorial Director: Caleb Pirtle III
Project Manager: Robyn Rogers
Creative Director: Kim Phillips

First Printing.

Manufactured in the United States of America.

Unless otherwise identified, all scripture quotations in this publication are taken from the New King James Version, copyright 1979, 1980, 1982, Thomas Nelson, Inc.

Scripture quotations marked TLB are taken from The Living Bible, 1971, Tyndale House Publishers.

Scripture quotations marked NIV are taken from the Holy Bible: New International Version, copyright 1973, 1978, 1984 by International Bible Society.

Contents

Dedication

Dedication

We lovingly dedicate this book to our children,
to their spouses, and to our grandchildren.
You have made our aging years pure joy.
We offer this book as part of our legacy to you.

To:
Jeffrey and Emily,
Trevor, Rentia, and Makenzie,
Vanessa, Greg, Macey, Kylee, Elijah, Jaden, Liberty,
and all the grandchildren yet to come.

Acknowledgments
Acknowledgments

Sincere thanks and appreciation to Randy Swanson for his direction
and guidance on this project, his financial expertise,
and all his other valuable input.

Thanks to Doug Brendel for his important contribution to this book
and his friendship through the years.

Thanks to Tara Duncan for her skillful editing and advice.

Thanks to Jill Muck for her research, her support, her willingness
to do whatever we needed, and as usual, her great attitude.

Thanks to John Thill for freely sharing his years of experience
and spiritual wisdom with us.

God bless you all. We could not have done it without you.

You're Never Too Old to Live Significantly

1. Actor George Burns won his first Oscar at age eighty.

2. Golda Meier was seventy-one when she became prime minister of Israel.

3. At age ninety-six playwright George Bernard Shaw broke his leg when he fell out of a tree he was trimming in his backyard.

4. Grandma Moses started painting at eighty years old. She completed more than 1,500 paintings after that; twenty-five percent of those were produced when she was past a hundred.

5. Michelangelo was seventy-one when he painted the Sistine Chapel.

6. Albert Schweitzer was still performing operations in his African hospital at age eighty-nine.

7. Doc Counsilman, at age fifty-eight, became the oldest person ever to swim the English Channel.

8. S.I. Hayakawa retired as president of San Francisco State University at seventy; then was elected to the U.S. Senate.

9. Casey Stengel didn't retire from managing the New York Mets until he was seventy-five.

10. Claude Monet, the greatest Impressionist painter, was still painting masterpieces in his eighties.

11. Pablo Picasso invented a new painting style in his seventies and painted until he died in his nineties.

12. Spanish cellist Pablo Casals planned to perform a new piece of music and practiced it on the very day he died at age ninety-seven.

13. James Michener wrote some of his best epic books after the age of sixty.

14. Ronald Reagan became president at the age of seventy.

The Search for Significance
A GPS to Guide You

*You will keep on guiding me all my life with your
wisdom and counsel; and afterwards receive me
into the glories of heaven!*

Psalm 73:24 (TLB)

Jerry

The average college freshman this year was born in 1988. That means for his entire life this has been his mindset:

- *The Soviet Union has never existed, so it's about as threatening as the student union.*
- *There has always been one Germany (not East and West).*
- *A coffee has always taken longer to make than a milkshake.*
- *Smoking has never been permitted on U.S. airlines.*
- *They have outgrown faxing as a means of communication.*
- *"Google" has always been a verb.*
- *Mr. Rogers, not Walter Cronkite, has always been the most trusted man in America.*
- *Bar codes have always been on retail products, mail, and library cards.*
- *They have rarely mailed anything using a stamp.*
- *Reality shows have always been on television. (Beloit College Mindset List)*

If you didn't feel old when you started reading, I'm sure you do now. Someone once said, "Inside every older person is a younger person wondering what in the world happened." I can relate to that.

Shirley and I have just completed thirty years of ministry in Chicago. Oh, what a difference thirty years can make. Check out these comparisons:

---

* *For clarity we have noted whether Jerry or Shirley is doing the writing at any given time.*

1976	**2006**
Long hair	*Longing for hair*
Acid rock	*Acid reflux*
Move to California because it's cool	*Move to California because it's warm*
Hoping for a BMW	*Hoping for a BM*
Going to a hip, new joint	*Receiving a new hip joint*
The Rolling Stones	*Kidney stones*
Pass the driver's test	*Pass the vision test*

I'm kidding, of course. But seriously, thirty years is a long time to spend in a job or ministry. I feel privileged to have been here, doing what God has called me to do. But many others look back on their careers as "merely making a living." They are looking to the second half of life as a time to do something significant.

The Search for Significance

Though I have been blessed to live out my passion and calling through my job, I have met many people who spend their entire careers making money, but never get the opportunity to do something really meaningful until retirement. Shirley and I met some young men who had made hundreds of millions of dollars during the dot com craze. Even though they eventually lost some of their fortunes, they were attending a gathering of people who were meeting specifically to explore ways to use their money to make a difference in the world and to leave a meaningful legacy to their children.

This desire for significance is not unusual. Even though many men and women have successful careers and some make a lot of money, as they begin to age they develop a passionate desire, not to retire, but to change direction and do something *significant* with the rest of their lives. They look at their final decades as a time for re-purposing. The bottom line is that status and power and money do not bring lasting satisfaction.

The problem is many do not know how to re-direct their lives toward significance. They need guidance. They need a roadmap. You might say they could use a Global Positioning System, or GPS, to give them direction for finding their own significance.

Global Positioning System

I have never owned a vehicle with a GPS, but I certainly have wished for one many times. With all the traveling I do, I have often found myself profoundly lost. If you are fortunate enough to have one of these amazing instruments, you may have wondered how it works.

Twenty-four satellites are continuously circling the earth, providing a signal by which we can electronically fix our location and our direction anywhere on the planet. The first satellite was launched in 1978. The current system is composed of a second generation of satellites started in 1989 called Block II. It is truly a marvel of modern technology. For less than a hundred dollars, anyone can buy a pocket-sized gadget that will tell you exactly where you are and how to get to any other point on the globe. As long as you have a GPS receiver and a clear view of the sky, you'll never be lost again.

The GPS system works on the principle of trilateration. A signal from three satellites is needed to fix your position. Let's say one signal tells you that you are 625 miles from Boise, Idaho. You could be anywhere on a circle that is 625 miles around Boise. Then another signal tells you that you are 690 miles from Minneapolis, Minnesota. These two circles would intersect each other at two points and you would be located at one of those two points. Now a third signal tells you that you are 615 miles from Tucson, Arizona. Those three circles will all intersect at only one point, Denver, Colorado. Three signals from three satellites can be used to identify your exact location on planet earth. That's pretty amazing stuff.

God's Plan for Significance

In the future chapters of this book, we will be looking at our own GPS. We call it *God's Plan for Significance*. Interestingly, it works in a similar fashion as the three satellites. Three critical issues help to define exactly where you are in life right now:

- *Your spiritual health,*
- *Your financial health,*
- *Your physical health.*

When these three spheres of life are in proper alignment, you can pinpoint your current position on your journey and chart your course for the rest of your life with a remarkable degree of accuracy. Like the satellites in space, God has provided His revealed Word, the Bible, and the Holy Spirit to be a continuous source of communication to us so that we can plot our position and our future course. Even your ultimate destination in eternity can be determined by using the signal sent from God for the benefit of finding your place and your way. If you love God and want to honor Him, God's plan can provide the global positioning for your own personal significance.

Shirley and I do not come to you as experts on aging, but rather as fellow travelers. As I write this chapter, my sixty-fifth birthday is just days away. (I know better than to mention Shirley's age.) For many, reaching retirement age is a milestone to look forward to. They anticipate retirement — a time to enjoy some well-deserved leisure, move to a warmer climate, take up a new hobby. For others, career has been the primary focus of life, and they approach retirement with something akin to panic — wondering what possible purpose their lives will hold now that their careers have come to a close.

Research shows that the more physically demanding and less intellectually stimulating an occupation, the sooner the worker will choose to retire, provided he or she can afford it. Judges, politicians, musicians and composers, religious workers, and college professors are among those who tend to stay in their jobs as long as they can. A lawyer or judge is seven times more likely to continue working past sixty-five than the average laborer. Now that mandatory retirement has ended, more and more workers are questioning when to retire or whether they should retire at all.[1]

As for me, I feel blessed to look upon my sixty-fifth birthday with some ambivalence and even indifference. I not only love my job, but consider it my calling and ministry. I don't intend to "retire" any time soon. That is, if retirement means stopping work. However, I do look forward to some positive transitions in the years ahead — a re-adjustment of responsibilities and job description. I prefer to look to my future as a "refirement" instead of retirement.

Following is a brief overview of my journey to this milestone and how my current ministry and calling could impact *your* future.

A Brief History

I have been an ordained minister for thirty years and a "preacher" since my teen years. During college, I felt a strong calling into Christian communications and television in particular. For more than forty years, God has allowed me the privilege to combine pulpit ministry with television. From a novice cameraman to set designer, to director, producer, lighting director, and finally into management, I have loved every moment I've spent in the industry. Studios and sound stages have always fascinated me, and even today when I walk into our television studios near Chicago, my pulse quickens and I feel a sense of excitement. I guess you might say television is in my blood. Not only has television been my career for over forty-five years, but the last thirty-three have been in *Christian* television. What a blessing it has been to marry this career I love to the advancement of God's kingdom.

Thirty years ago, Shirley and I came to Chicago to put a fledgling television station on the air. A local pastor, Owen Carr, felt called by God to begin a TV station to reach the millions in the vast Chicagoland area. Through his great faith and the generosity of his congregation, Channel 38 was purchased. But not only did the infant TV station have no license, almost no money, and no employees, Owen knew nothing about television. So he contacted me in Virginia where I was working with Pat Robertson at CBN and asked if I would come and put TV38 on the air. Shirley and I felt strongly that God was leading us here, but we could never have imagined the amazing journey that awaited us.

We left a comfortable and familiar life in the South to embark on the biggest faith venture of our lives in the concrete jungle of Chicago — bitterly cold weather, strange-sounding people, high rise condos with locked doors, and a job with no guarantees. Through a series of small and not-so-small miracles, TV38 signed on the air in 1976. I served as vice president and general manager until 1979 when Owen moved on to other areas of ministry and I became president.

For twenty-two years, we were a local broadcast station that served primarily the Chicagoland area. In order to expand our ministry and have the ability to focus more on developing relevant programming that would reach our post-modern culture, we eventually sold the local station and became the Total Living Network. The details of the remarkable history of TV38 and TLN is recorded in my book *Deep Faith for Dark Valleys* (Thomas Nelson Publishers).

God has blessed TV38 and later TLN these past three decades. Today, we have cable channels in Chicago and San Francisco, broadcast stations in Illinois and Nevada, and a 24-hour satellite channel. Most importantly, we have become content providers. We produce documentaries, series, specials, Shirley's women's show, and other programs and films. These programs minister to and educate the community not only on our stations, but on others around the country and even internationally. Our outreach has expanded from a relatively small local audience to a global market.

Thirty years ago, before the explosion of technology, broadcast television and movie theaters were the only ways to see a video image. Today, along with broadcast, there is cable, satellite, the internet, VCR's, videos, DVD's, Direct TV, video games, Ipods, and cell phones. And I have been right in the middle of it all, heart racing, eyes wide with wonder, running to keep up.

It has been an incredible journey of faith, adversity, mountain tops and valleys, victories, mistakes, and joyful fulfillment. God has been very good to me. My wife Shirley has been my partner and encourager through thirty-nine years of marriage and has shared every exciting moment of our Chicago experience. She is a prime example of someone who blossomed later in life and who is maximizing her "second half." Here is a little of her story.

Aspiring Women and Other Surprises

Recently, as I sat on the beautiful *Aspiring Women* television set, I had one of life's "defining moments." The full impact of what I was doing hit me. I thought *Am I awake; is this real?*

Each week, I appear on television with my two friends and co-hosts, Michelle McKinney Hammond and Tammy Maltby. TLN produces *Aspiring Women*, a program that features women who have overcome some of life's most devastating setbacks to live lives of triumph. Our women's stories send out a message of encouragement to those in every state across the U.S. and many countries overseas. And to top it off, we have a great time doing it! I asked myself, *Does it get any better than this?*

I give God all the glory for the success of this show because *Aspiring Women* came as rather a surprise to me when I was fifty years old! A production committee at TLN was revamping our program schedule and wanted several new programs. They asked anyone who had an idea to submit it. I had worked on air with Jerry from time to time, but never had any strong aspirations to be an on-air personality. I spoke to women's groups frequently, and this was enough "on stage" time for me. However, I secretly had an idea rolling around in my head for a women's show, so I turned in my idea to the committee. To my (and Jerry's) surprise, they decided to produce the show and asked me to be one of the co-hosts. We chose Tammy and Michelle to join me, and the rest, as they say, is history. God has blessed this program beyond my wildest expectations. *Aspiring Women* has won numerous awards and several nominations for Emmy's in the Chicago market. Several years later, it is still going strong. And perhaps the greatest blessing is that it is broadcast all over the Middle East, Europe, and even into the Far East through SAT 7 satellites.

My next milestone came when I decided to write my first book at age fifty-three. I had written many articles and edited books, but never had the courage to try a book of my own. I decided to take many of the teachings and messages I had presented to women over the years and compile a teaching book. *Growing Your Dreams* was accepted by a small but wonderful publishing company, and though the writing was not that good, it was my entrée into a very difficult field.

Now on my fifth book, I know without a doubt that writing is one of my principal callings in the second half of my life. I plan to write as long as I can. As anyone in the industry can tell you, writing is great, but publishing books can be the most painful, heart-wrenching roller coaster of any job I know. Publishing keeps me humble and totally dependent on the Lord. Through its many frustrations, it has stretched me and caused me to grow. But it gives me joy, fulfillment, and purpose, too. My writing and my TV program are great examples of what can happen in the second half of life if we have faith in God and the courage to pursue our dreams.

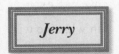

Jerry

All these years, I have focused on the combination of ministry and television, and little else excited me. But when I heard about an association called Significant Living the lights went on. I not only saw the answer to my own concerns about aging, but I also saw how this membership organization could help others find their way to personal significance.

While the concept of Significant Living (SL) held great interest, the potential of *combining* TLN and Significant Living excited me even more. The synergy was perfect. SL offers a vitally important message to the huge group of Americans in the second half of life. With TLN's state of the art television studios, broadcast and satellite capabilities, cable channels, national and international teleconferencing potential, program syndication, and distribution network, we have the ability to get that vital message to the aging community worldwide. I am convinced that God has brought Significant Living and TLN together for this time in history to serve the dominant, over-fifty population and direct them to their greatest personal potential in Christ. Working together, we truly have the opportunity to impact our world.

Shirley and I, along with TLN, have launched this organization and written this book to help you enjoy and maximize the second half of your life. Through books such as this one, speaking, conferences, a video library, missions trips, TV programs, and more, we want to provide resources for the inevitable challenges and opportunities that come with aging. But more importantly, we seek to help you discover your own significance in light of God's plan for you.

Yes, this book is definitely for you *Baby Boomers*, those of you born between 1946 and 1964. But it is also for those of us who are well past our sixtieth birthdays. With unprecedented good health and longevity, we can expect to live two to three more decades. All of us must come to grips with what we will do with the rest of our lives. We have tried to provide *information* and *inspiration* that you can turn to again and again in your quest for true significance. It is our prayer that this book will become a tool in God's hand, a roadmap — or better yet a positioning system, a GPS, to guide you to your destination. Your journey's not over; for many, it's just beginning.

You cannot fully appreciate the importance of this message at this unique moment in history unless you understand the changing era in which we live. Something massive is on the horizon — a phenomenon unprecedented in history. And it presents an enormous opportunity to minister to a huge demographic of people — the aging American. Let's take a look at what's happening in this world of ours.

Suggested Reading

Suggested Reading

Deep Faith for Dark Valleys, Jerry Rose
Shattered Dreams, Larry Crab

Chuckles

Patient: How can I live to be a hundred?
Doctor: Give up cookies, cake, and ice cream. Stop eating red meat, potatoes, and bread.
Patient: If I do that, I'll live to be a hundred?
Doctor: Maybe not, but it will certainly seem like it.

After a serious operation, the woman was still unconscious. Her worried husband stood at the foot of her bed.
"Well," said the nurse reassuringly, "at least age is on her side."
"She's not so young," said the husband. "She's forty-five."
At this point, the patient moved slightly and murmured softly but firmly, "forty-four."

A reporter asked a man on his ninety-fifth birthday, "To what do you credit your long life?"
"Not sure yet," replied the old-timer. "My lawyer is negotiating with two breakfast cereal companies."

I adore my bifocals,
My false teeth fit fine,
My hairpiece looks good,
But I sure miss my mind.

Old man: This new hearing aid is fantastic. I couldn't hear this good even when I was a kid. I've never had better hearing.
Old woman: What kind is it?
Old man: A quarter till five.

When I was young, there was no respect for the young,
And now that I'm old, there is no respect for the old.
I missed out coming and going. (J. B. Priestley)

The senior told his friend, "We went to a great restaurant last night. Good food, cheap prices."
His friend asked, "What's the name?"
Scratching his head, the senior replied: "Oh, the name? I can't remember. Uh …what's the name of that flower? It has a long stem and a red flower?"
"A rose?"
"Yes! Hey, Rose, what's the name of that restaurant we went to last night?"

A Whole New World

The Age Wave and Other Generational Phenomena

...I have created you and cared for you since you were born.
I will be your God through all your lifetime, yes, even when
your hair is white with age. I made you and I will care for you...

Isaiah 46:3, 4 (TLB)

Jerry

Those of us in the second half of life, who I like to refer to as "second halfers," make up the largest population demographic in the history of America. We are the sons and daughters of what has been described as "The Greatest Generation." Our fathers and mothers fought two wars and saved the world from tyranny. They were hard workers, humble people who believed in an honest days work. They saved and built for a positive future for their families. They were, for the most part, people of strong faith and solid character — and they left us a great heritage.

Our generation has enjoyed and benefited from the freedom they gave us. But we have had our own challenges, our own wars, and our own successes and failures. We are a generation of risk takers and achievers. During the past fifty years, we have experienced an explosion of innovation, creativity, and new ideas — from Space to Silicon Valley.

Think about it. These two generations have witnessed everything from the first flight at Kitty Hawk to the first walk on the moon. From the structured family life of the Ozzie Nelson family to the startling dysfunction of the Ozzie Osborne family.

As youngsters, we survived a world without seat belts, air bags, or baby seats. There were no child proof medicine bottles, cell phones, video games, or Internet. No cable or satellite. We played outside and even went to the park with friends without our parents having to watch to ensure our protection.

A service station was just that — a place where an attendant not only filled your car with gas, but cleaned your windshield and checked your oil and tire pressure. And all those extras were free. We harnessed solar power and survived flower power. I think it could well be said that we are a generation that has "been there and done that." But now we are entering another season of life — the second half, or the aging years. And we will have plenty of company.

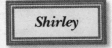

Shirley

America is definitely getting older. But today's "seniors" are not what they used to be. In fact, most older adults, myself included, dislike the term "senior." We don't look, act, or think as "seniors" once did. I'd like to begin with the story of our *mature* friend Jill Muck. She is *not* your typical grandmother — yet her story is becoming more and more common. As we'll see, the term "senior" is taking on a whole new connotation, putting on a brand new face.

Not Your Mother's Grandmother

Jill is a cute, sassy, green-eyed blond who enjoys exercise and has always been crazy about martial arts. When a course in self-defense was offered in her neighborhood, she just had to go. She persuaded her twelve-year-old daughter Melissa to go with her. Melissa liked the class, but Jill *loved* it.

The class in Tae Kwon Do was composed of mostly kids who started with the customary beginner's white belt. But there was one other woman who had earned a green belt. So Jill, always competitive, was determined to earn a *black* belt. She went on to an even greater achievement, a First Degree Black Belt. Guess how old she was when she reached this milestone. She was fifty! But that was only the beginning.

Tae Kwon Do gave her a tremendous feeling of accomplishment. She found the sport both mentally and physically challenging. Though it's one of the scariest things she ever did, Jill thinks this achievement was the beginning of her liberation.

Jill and her husband Ron had a nice life, raising their three children in a Chicago suburb. Jill didn't have a job back then, but did a lot of volunteer work. When her children were grown, Jill joined her childhood friend's recruiting firm. It was at this company where someone introduced her to Jesus, and she says her life just exploded. She began a God-given adventure that is still going strong today.

She and her friend later became partners in an international import/export business. Unfortunately, the business ended rather suddenly, which left Jill feeling at loose ends and wondering what she would do with herself. She had always felt a little insecure because she hadn't gone to college. When her girlfriends talked of their experiences at the university and the fun of sororities, she felt she had missed out on too much.

So at the age of fifty-seven, Jill went back to school — DePaul University's School for New Learning. All the students in the program are over twenty-three, but Jill was among the oldest. She decided to get the hardest courses over with first, so to the horror of her family, she signed up for physics and algebra! Not being a math person, and not having gone to school in forty years, she was obviously in way over her head. But her family helped, she hired tutors, and she not only passed the courses, but made two A's!

At the same time Jill was going to school full-time in the evenings, she took a part-time job during the day, working for the prestigious Monsanto/NutraSweet Corporation. The job eventually became full time, and Jill worked for one of the company's top physicians, the doctor who headed up clinical research. Monsanto was willing to reimburse Jill's tuition bills if they were job-related, so Jill went on to earn a Bachelor of Arts in International Operations and Management and had her entire education underwritten by Monsanto. Jill received her degree at the age of sixty-one!

Getting her education was truly life-changing for this grandmother. It gave her a confidence she had never known. But she also realizes that degrees don't make her more valuable or more worthy as a person. She understands that her real worth lies in what God has done for her.

Today, Jill is near seventy, but she's still a cute, trim, sassy blonde with those same disarming green eyes. And even though she doesn't participate in martial arts anymore, she still loves exercise and staying fit. She's now writing a book with her childhood friend and partner about their globe-trotting adventures. One of her many goals is to get the book published during her lifetime.

Jill certainly blows away the image of the sedentary, graying grandmother in a rocking chair, filling her days with knitting and napping. And in this new world of ours, that image is probably gone forever. But before we get to the "new seniors," let's consider the group that is literally taking over this country by their sheer numbers alone: the *Baby Boomers*.

Baby Boomers

Most everyone is aware by now of the generation called the *Baby Boomers*. They are the largest demographic in U.S. history, the group of babies born between 1946 and 1964. (Some sources use the dates 1943 to 1960.) This mass of people, some seventy-six million, has dominated American culture for five decades. Every eight seconds, one of these "babies" is entering the second half of life. In the next decade, thousands will turn fifty every single day! *(BBHQ: Boomer Statistics)*

Why are there so many boomers? Well, the obvious post-war explanation is that after World War II, when things returned to normal, births rose dramatically in many parts of the world. This phenomenon was partly due to the widespread optimism and soaring economy that came with the war's end. And, of course, the other reason is that when the boys returned home, they made up for lost time in the romance department. What is surprising is that in most countries this birth spurt lasted for three to six years. But for some unknown reason, in the United States, Canada, Australia, and New Zealand, the boom lasted for two decades![1]

What distinguishes the boomers from their parents and grandparents? They grew up in a whole new world. They were coming into their own during the sixties. The boomers made up the anti-war, free love, hippie idealists. Unlike their stable, hard-working parents, they focused on education and working smarter. They challenged the system on every level. While they rejected the church at large, they believed their generation possessed a unique vision, a moral acuity more precise than anything in the history of mankind.[2]

The aging boomer, hippie turned yuppie, eventually came to appreciate the rewards of the establishment they had once rejected. Boomers remain rather self-focused and materialistic. They are life-long learners. They take better care of themselves. They are still idealists, and, as they age, they are strongly motivated to do something significant. They have a great need to leave a legacy to their children.

The most important thing for us to consider regarding the boomers is their continued influence. In fact, boomers have impacted their environment from birth forward. And that impact has flowed over to adjacent generations, both those preceding them and those who follow. Consequently, the boomer phenomenon affects all of us, no matter our age. It is interesting to see how that influence began and how it has continued.

When the boomers arrived, the diaper and baby food industry prospered. As the boomers suffered scraped knees and runny noses, a huge pediatric, medical enterprise arose, and Dr. Spock became an icon. When they started school in the '50s, elementary schools had to be expanded. More elementary schools, high schools, and colleges were built in the '50s, '60s, and '70s, respectively, than at any other time.

With the enlightenment of higher education, media awareness of international conflicts, and the first taste of freedom, social unrest and political rebellion erupted on campuses across the country. Rebellion in teens and early twenty-year-olds is common, but when seventy-six million young people rebel at the same time, you have a revolution.

What will happen as the boomers turn forty and fifty? What will a mid-life crisis look like when it is multiplied by seventy-six million? This group is, above all, the "youth" generation. Their love of youth has shaped our culture and economy. The explosion in health clubs, jogging shoes, supplements, cosmetic surgery, and hair transplants prove they plan to grow old gracefully, slowly, and youthfully.[3] I must admit as an older boomer, I am right there with them. The boomers have flexed their muscles throughout their entire lives and will continue to shape the political and social landscape of America for decades to come.

Dr. Ken Dychtwald calls the aging of America the *Age Wave*. Charles and

Win Arn call it the approaching *Tsunami.* Closer examination of the *Age Wave* reveals that millions of aging boomers are not the only reason older Americans outnumber the young by such a huge margin. Dychtwald points out that the lack of balance in age groups is also caused by two other important changing demographics: the *Senior Boom* and the *Birth Dearth.*[4]

The Senior Surge

Do you realize that two-thirds of all persons sixty-five or older who have *ever* lived are alive today? In 1776, a child born in America could expect to live to about age thirty-five. A century later, life expectancy was about age forty. Early Americans didn't have to worry about how to handle old age or care for aging parents because their parents were already gone by the time they reached what we would consider middle age. They didn't have to concern themselves with how they would handle the empty nest since it would generally be empty for about eighteen months before their death. There was no such thing as Social Security or Medicare; there were simply very few old people.

The last century has brought extraordinary breakthroughs in health care and the elimination of disease. Diseases such as cholera, tuberculosis, typhoid, and diphtheria rarely take the lives of Americans. Even AIDS, which is expected to claim nearly two million lives in the next decade, pales in comparison to diseases like the bubonic plague and influenza that killed tens of millions worldwide in past centuries. Consider these current realities:

- *In the decades since 1900, approximately thirty years have been added to the average life expectancy in this country.*
- *The Census Bureau projects that life expectancy in 2040 will be seventy-five years for men and eighty-three for women. The National Institute on Aging projects eighty-six years for men and ninety-one and a half years for women.*[5]
- *In the next eighty years, the centenarian population will increase by seventy-five times!*

• *In the year 2000, fourteen percent of the population was over sixty-five. It is predicted that by 2020 it will rise to seventeen percent.*
• *By 2040, a full twenty-five percent of Americans will be over sixty-five!*[6]

Marketplace trends demonstrate clearly that the years ahead will be marked by a severe shortage of workers. And with young people representing a lower percentage of the population, older workers will find themselves in greater demand. Companies will think less about mandatory retirement and begin to search for ways to retain older employees.

What do these statistics mean to you and me? It means that for the rest of our lives, the population will be dominated by boomers and older adults. We will not only be living longer, we will be living healthier. Our bodies will be more active and so will our minds. And like our friend Jill, this age group will be radically different from previous generations in terms of finances, health, activity, and productivity.

The Arns suggest that the best way to understand today's seniors is to throw out everything you think you know about this group. Most of these folks do not think of themselves as old or declining. They don't think, act, or dress like the traditional stereotype. Few of them would attend a "senior citizens" group or "senior" Sunday School class. They reject terms such as "primetimers," "Golden Agers," or "elder" anything. This huge crowd has claimed the territory of "middle adults." The group extends from fifty plus to at least seventy.

They view the future as a time of harvest and renewal rather than a time of winter and retreat. They are focused on the present, not the past, on serving rather than being served, on working rather than resting. They want to learn, to grow, and yes, to play.[7]

As this group of adults zooms past retirement age, they expect not only to be around for decades to come, but to be influencers and contributors, changing their world. They are a force to be reckoned with. Today's seniors have had a tremendous impact on American life. They will continue to affect all aspects of society: politics, the economy, the housing market, and most of all, the attitude toward aging.

So the aging of America has come about not only because of the baby boom, but also because of the senior surge. You may wonder how long this age imbalance will continue. There is no end in sight — due to the third changing demographic, the *birth dearth.*

The Birth Dearth

The only way to re-balance the aging population would be a significant increase in births. That birth increase is just not happening. Unlike previous generations, the *Baby Boomers* have gotten married later in life or remained single. Those boomers who have married have produced fewer offspring than previous generations. It is estimated that twenty percent of boomers have no children and twenty-five percent have only one.

There are many reasons for this birthrate decline. One reason is financial. As the cost of living and raising children has increased, each child represents tremendous long-term costs. As more women work, children become more expensive. A mother must either forego a paycheck to stay home with the children or apply most of her salary toward daycare. Another reason is family instability. As the divorce rate goes up, fewer adults are willing to risk putting children in an unstable environment. A third reason cited for fewer births is a sense that the world is a scary place. As the threat of nuclear war and terrorist attacks increase, some are reluctant to put future children at such risk.[8] Consequently, the baby boom has been replaced by a birth dearth. The increased longevity of the population along with low fertility has changed the age balance indefinitely. The focus of our society is moving from youth to the aging, and this tilt will not change in our lifetime.

You may be asking, "Now that we have this information, what does it mean to us personally? How will the coming *Age Wave* impact us as Americans and as Christians?" These are the questions we will address throughout the remainder of this book. Like you, Jerry and I are grappling with both the global and the personal impacts of aging. It is our goal that you begin to examine these questions in relation to your future. The answers to these questions may be as individual as each person who answers, but we hope our personal sharing will get you started. Next, Jerry and I will share some of our own personal realizations about aging. See if you can relate.

A Time of Transitions

I have been active in a large organization, National Religious Broadcasters, for thirty years. I served as its president for three years. Each year at the NRB convention, I network with other broadcasters and programmers and leaders in the industry. It is a great time to learn, as well as to teach the young Christian broadcasters coming along behind me.

Last year a young woman came up to me and said, "Mr. Rose, it is such an honor to meet you. I consider you one of the pioneers in religious broadcasting."

Pioneer! I must say I was taken aback. It seems just a few years ago I was being called a "young Turk," and now I am a "pioneer." How the time flies. It was only one of many reminders that I am aging.

While turning sixty-five is really not a big deal to me, I must admit to physical changes I can no longer deny or ignore. One is the power of gravity on my body. Enough said. And I reluctantly admit to some physical limitations. I just don't do some things as well as I used to. When our company had a ball game the other day, they put me in the infield. I can hold my own at pitching, catching, and batting. But perhaps the wise captain didn't think I'd be as good at running for fly balls as I used to be.

A few months ago, I was at a Western theme park in Arizona with my family.

My son-in-law clearly outrode me on a mechanical bull. What is that about? I am the Texan, the cowboy, and the horse person. Well, it's about aging.

I am happy to say, however, that at my age there are many things I do better. I am wiser and hopefully have better judgment. I can put to good use the wealth of experience I have gained in my field over four decades. Shirley and I are empty nesters and have enjoyed having more freedom and more choices. Yes, my body is declining, but my mind and my opportunities are growing. I don't want to slow down; I want to re-focus. I want to develop a plan for the second half of life that will allow me to continue to have a fulfilling life for God, others, and myself. And yet, all of us in the second half of life face changes and challenges. Aging is a time of transitions.

Shirley

I can appreciate the good parts of aging. I'm not sure I'd want to be thirty again (but maybe forty or forty-five). I am a better person today than I was as a young person. I have become wiser, more sensitive, more compassionate, and more patient over the years. One thing I like better about my older self is my confidence. I no longer wrestle with the self-doubt and the misplaced insecurities of my youth. Yes, with the passing years we learn some valuable life lessons. Many of us, over time, have become better acquainted with our Savior and Lord. This deepening relationship is perhaps the best part of aging.

Oh, I know it's not all good. I don't like the aches and pains. I hate the new wrinkles I see on my face. I resist the fact that I don't have the stamina I once had. The heels on my shoes are lower (no more stilettos for me). My waistline has grown, and I have an impressive wardrobe of elastic garments. No matter how much I exercise, belly fat and cellulite are constant realities. And when did my legs begin to resemble a map of Illinois? And I can totally relate to Jerry's comment about gravity.

But it isn't just this body that's changing. Physical decline is *not* the most difficult part of aging. Our house is now silent much of the time. Being alone doesn't mean being lonely, but there are times when I am. Holidays are different than they were when the children were still at home. Yes, we often spend holidays with our kids out of town. But it's not the same as when our home was the gathering place and center of activity. I miss those times. I miss the noise. I miss the clutter. I miss the cooking. I miss the loved ones.

Though we resist change, it's a part of life. Everyone that has lived fifty years knows nothing ever stays the same very long. Transitions are part of living and growing and certainly part of aging. But even though change often puts us way out of our comfort zone, it's not always a bad thing.

As I look back, I can remember several painful transitions in our younger years. When our two sons were five and three years old, we moved from Dallas to Virginia. We felt strongly it was God's will for our family, but it was a difficult move. We left Jerry's parents who lived nearby. They had been very close to our children. We left dear friends. We left our church. We left Texas (just shy of heaven in my husband's opinion). And the Virginia experience wasn't ideal. But looking back, we can see it was a change we needed to make. It prepared us for our ministry here in Chicago.

For twenty years, we attended a wonderful church in Chicago. We loved our pastor; he was one of my husband's closest friends. Then suddenly Pastor Bob died at age fifty-six. We were devastated. It was terribly painful to walk into church and see his seat empty.

Shortly afterward, my daughter, her husband, and my two grandchildren moved away. Sunday morning services that had once been times of joyous worship and fellowship became sad and gloomy. It was so different without our kids and our beloved pastor. We hated the change.

Before long, my husband was asked to serve as associate pastor for a small country church. A few months earlier, I doubt if we would even have considered it. But now it seemed exactly what we needed to do. God has blessed us and used

Jerry's ministry at our little church.

Change is usually uncomfortable and often painful. But looking back, I can see God's faithful hand in each situation. The agony of loss and the challenge of creating a "new normal" have caused me to lean harder on the Lord and trust Him more. I have seen blessings evolve in spite of each painful adjustment.

The second half of life *always* brings change. It is the season of transitions. Perhaps you are *struggling* with an empty nest, or you may be *loving* it. But letting your offspring go is never easy. You may be dealing with aging parents. You may have discovered one of life's greatest joys, grandchildren, and are experiencing the changes these little ones bring with them. Perhaps you are approaching retirement with a conflict of emotions, knowing it will be a huge transition. But even though change is never easy, it is often the best thing for us. It all depends on our flexibility and how we view the transitions.

Jerry

Retirement is not a popular word today. There is a new notion of what it means to "retire." Most of us will not be willing to hang up all the knowledge and experience we have gained over the years and "retire" to the sidelines. There is too much living ahead to do that. Being an aging adult does not mean the *conclusion* of a meaningful, productive life, but rather the *beginning* of a new and exciting season of life.

Perhaps 'transition" is a better word to describe our new season. That transition can include a lot of things: travel, adventure, life-long learning, healthy choices through better diet, and exercise. It can mean financial stability through good planning and stewardship principles. But perhaps most importantly, it means the opportunity to discover a level of significance greater than anything we've experienced before. Yet some view retirement as a negative and approach it with anxiety or fear.

I crossed the path of a gentleman at the Union League Club in Chicago. He had been forced to retire, and as a result, his life was effectively over. As we sat and talked, his bitterness poured out. He deeply resented being forced out of his company, and he simply had nothing else going in his life. I know he was financially well off. He had made all the money he would ever need. He simply couldn't get past the loss of his career.

His career had become such a huge part of his life that he literally had no other identity. No interests. He had been completely stripped of everything he felt he had worked for. He was no longer needed, and now he was basically just hanging around, waiting to die. I tried to help him realize that there were positive aspects to his situation. But he couldn't find them. He got angry at me; he was determined to be a victim. How sad that this gentleman couldn't see the opportunity, hadn't made a plan for his future. Yes, a change in our careers or work can be very difficult, but we don't have to be defined by our work alone.

When my father retired, he simply stopped working. He didn't have a good plan for the rest of his life. He had worked for the city of Dallas in a blue-collar job for his whole working life. So he had looked forward to a time of leisure and relaxation. But when my mother retired a few months later, the fireworks began.

Both mom and dad had been in the work force for years. Though they loved each other dearly, their relationship had at times been stormy. But most of their daytime hours had been spent away from each other. With both of them retiring at the same time, they were together the better part of twenty-four hours a day. They not only had no plan for what to do with their retirement time, they didn't have a plan about what to do together. My mom felt claustrophobic with dad in the house all day. Dad wanted her there with him most of the time. Mom became responsible for most of the care of my grandmother, and dad was angry that other relatives weren't helping.

Dad had never had a great relationship with mom's bachelor brother, and now since she had retired the brother would just "happen by" on a regular basis, especially around meal time. By the time my mom called me, she and my father were nearing the end of their rope. Shirley and I lived in Chicago, so I flew home to Texas, determined to help them sort through the difficulties and build a plan for surviving retirement.

The first thing we did was talk about what each one of them expected out of retirement. Mom wanted space, and Dad wanted to be with her. Mom wanted to be a caregiver, and Dad wanted the family to share the load in both time and money. Mom wanted her brother to feel at home at their house, and Dad wanted him to feel more at home at his *own* house. During the next three days, we spent a lot of time talking and negotiating our way through the struggles. We set some parameters on being together and having the freedom of personal space. We met with relatives and agreed on some cooperation in the care of their mother. I scheduled a meeting with my uncle and Dad, and the three of us worked through their relationship problem. There was fault on both sides, and, by the end of the meeting, they had asked each other's forgiveness. At the end of three days, there was at least the framework for a better relationship during the "autumn years."

It wasn't perfect, and the "autumn years" still produced a few storms, but my mother and father loved each other, and they made it through with the relationship intact. I remember what a hole there was in my dad's heart after my mother died. On more than one occasion when I visited him in Texas, he talked about how he looked forward to being with her again. But their retirement had seriously impacted their relationship.

Shirley

The most difficult changes brought about by aging are often in relationships. Even if you have not yet retired, you may be dealing with a daughter- or son-in-law for the first time. One of your children may have gotten a divorce, and you're afraid of losing your grandchildren or struggling to relate to the estranged parent.

What about your relationship with your spouse? You may, like Jerry's mother and father, have to manage much more together time. You might suddenly wake up one day and realize you're sharing your bed with a stranger. After decades of marriage, you feel the distance between you and wonder about the future. Hopefully, your marriage has gotten stronger, but as empty nesters you must adjust your way of relating to one another and re-think your priorities.

One thing is sure: relationships are not static. They ebb and flow. There are seasons of harmony and times of tension and stress. Disagreements, misunderstandings, and hurt feelings do not go away with maturity. Our lives and relationships usually become more complicated as the years go by.

But the good news is that our relationships *can* grow stronger. New friendships can be built. Our lives can become far richer and more joyful. Whatever work it takes to protect and nourish these relationships is well worth the effort. Our marriages can be better than ever. Our adult children and in-laws can become our best friends. And we can be a godly influence on our children and grandchildren. Developing healthy relationships is one sure way of living significantly.

Success vs. Significance

Jerry

What is significance anyway? The dictionary defines significant as "having or likely to have a major effect; important; fairly large in amount or quantity." Some people get significance confused with success. They are cousins but not identical twins. I think all of us want to be significant in every season of our lives. But what does that look like? The answer is different for each one of us.

In the classic movie *It's a Wonderful Life*, George, who is played by Jimmy Stewart, thinks his life has been insignificant because he hasn't been successful in the same way as his brother. His life, in comparison, seems drab and mundane. But he learns, over the course of the movie, just how significant he's been — how much difference he's made in the world.

For some, significance may come through mentoring or having a positive influence on the family. It may be starting a business or doing volunteer work. It is not so important whether we do something small or big. The importance lies in filling a need in the lives of other people. Significance usually translates into getting involved with others.

Harold is seventy-two and Patty is in her fifties. They have a large family of biological and adopted children and are pretty cramped living in an old farmhouse in northern Wisconsin. When someone gave them a large financial gift, they decided to build their dream home on the property. But they were only in the home five months when a tragic fire completely destroyed the house. Instead of rebuilding, they used the insurance settlement to open an orphanage in Liberia and are helping Americans adopt these very needy children.

Les, a literary agent, spent a successful career in the publishing business. In their seventies, Les and his wife felt called to move away from their home, children, and grandchildren in Massachusetts to minister in a horse community in North Carolina. They have had a successful and rewarding ministry there, focused in and through a church. They have a lovely home and more property than they ever could have had in the Northeast. And, by the way, Les has more business as an agent than ever before.

There are infinite numbers of ways we can find our own significance. No one can tell you what that looks like. It's up to you — fully yielded to God's plan — to discover your own significance. But I believe in God's reality *significance* equals *obedience*.

In the 20th chapter of the book of Numbers, the nation of Israel found themselves in a wilderness desert without water — a nation of thirsty people, venting their frustration on Moses, their leader. Moses, unlike the children of Israel, remembered God's miracle-working power. So he went to God for an answer, and God gave him one. God told him to speak to the rock and water would pour forth.

The direction was clear, and Moses was confident it would happen. However, in his anger at the people for their complaining, Moses struck the rock instead of speaking to it. Water poured forth anyway. The people drank and their thirst was quenched. Praise replaced the complaints. Suddenly Moses was back in the good graces of the crowd. He was "God's man of the hour" again.

But there was one problem. What looked like success was really a failure. Moses had disobeyed God. God said, "Speak to the rock," but Moses had struck it. Some would say, "But it worked! So it must be okay!" But it wasn't. Disobedience to God's will is never acceptable. Moses soon discovered how serious God really was about obedience. Because of Moses' disobedience, God didn't allow him to enter into the Promised Land.

The foundation to finding God's plan for significance is obedience. Obedience is far more important than sacrifice, good works, or anything else. Success does not automatically mean obedience, and it does not equal significance. We are responsible for obedience — God is responsible for any success we may encounter. But when we are obedient, significance always follows.

Neither I nor anyone can dictate what significance means to you. I believe the aging years can be the most productive and fruitful and satisfying season of our lives — when we discover God's will for those years. It's not a mystery, and it is not difficult. But there are several important principals that will help you on the road to significance. In the following chapters, we will share what we believe to be some of these necessary points to guide you to your destination.

To summarize, our world has changed forever because of the great numbers of aging Americans. The "new seniors" and "middle adult boomers" are more active and healthier, live longer, and are more ambitious for significance than any previous generations. Yet, success does not equal significance; significance usually translates into obedience to God.

As you read, prayerfully consider how you can make positive changes in your life that will result in a future of joy, influence, fruitfulness, and fulfillment. Let's begin the journey.

Suggested Reading

The Age Wave, Ken Dychtwald, Ph.D. and Joe Flower

The New Senior, Charles Arn and Win Arn

Second Wind for the Second Half, Patrick Morley

How to Retire Happy, Stan Hinden

The Baby Boomer's Guide to Getting it Right the Second Time Around, Gary Null, Ph.D. with Vicki Riba Koestler

I'm the Same Old Me

When I was in my younger days, I weighed a few pounds less,
I needn't hold my tummy in to wear a belted dress.

But now that I am older, I've set my body free;
There's the comfort of elastic where once my waist would be.

Inventor of those high heeled shoes, my feet have not forgiven;
I have to wear a nine now, but I used to wear a seven.

And how about those pantyhose — they're sized by weight, you see,
So how come when I put them on the crotch is at my knee?

I need to wear these glasses as the print's been getting smaller;
And it wasn't very long ago I know that I was taller.

Though my hair has turned to gray and my skin no longer fits,
On the inside, I'm the same old me, it's the outside's changed a bit.

The Senility Prayer

God grant me the senility
to forget the people I never liked;
The good fortune to run into the ones I do,
And the eyesight to tell the difference.

First Coordinate:
Attitude
Developing a Godly Perspective on Aging

For God did not give us a spirit of timidity, but a spirit of power, of love and of self-discipline.

2 Timothy 1:7 (NIV)

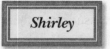

Shirley

As Jerry approached his fiftieth birthday, he needed an attitude adjustment. He was being a real stinker. As president of a Christian organization, he rightly assumed his staff would want to honor his birthday. He wouldn't have any part of it.

He informed his secretary and me in no uncertain terms: he did not want any "over the hill" parties. He would not find it amusing. He was the boss, and that was that. I knew in part why he was being so uncharacteristically negative. He had just lost his mother to cancer, and his dad had entered a nursing home. He was still grieving and feeling much like an orphan. His fiftieth birthday just arrived at a bad time.

Even so, I wasn't going to let him get away with that attitude. I sat him down, and we had a serious talk. I reminded him of his own battle with cancer ten years earlier. How God had intervened and spared his life. I pointed out how close he had come to never reaching his fiftieth birthday. I made it clear I would not allow any more whining. He had been blessed with life, and there was indeed a reason for celebration. It worked. His attitude and perspective changed as he realized reaching fifty is a good thing. It is a gift that many are not given.

Did I honor his wishes about a party? Ah … no. As Jerry walked into our TV studio on his birthday, dozens of guests greeted him. His party was even broadcast live on television. There were surprise guests from his childhood, television colleagues, and video greetings from many around the country. It was definitely an "over the hill" that was way over the top. And by the way, Jerry loved every minute of it. It was a great example of what a difference it makes to have the right attitude about aging.

Our friend John Thill has worked with seniors for years and often speaks at aging seminars. He frequently begins his seminar with the question, "How would you define successful aging?"

Many of the attendees have never had to put a definition into words, and many have either consciously or subconsciously avoided the issue altogether. He receives an interesting array of answers such as:

- *"I don't want a definition, because I'm not going there."*
- *"I don't know." (One of the more honest answers.*
- *"Stay young, stay fit, stay engaged, stay in contact with others, stay positive, stay in my own home, stay free, stay rich." (Notice the answers center around "stay.")*
- *"Don't get old, don't lose control, don't smoke, don't go to a nursing home, don't give up, don't get stuck in the past." (Notice the answers center around "don't.")*
- *"Stay young, act young, be young at heart." (And my personal favorite) "Stay as young as you can for as long as you can and die quick!" (Many of these definitions center around "young.")*

The definitions reveal a great deal about the prevailing attitude on aging. Could many of us simply be in denial? Someone has suggested that if our goal is to "stay young," it would be like telling a child to be an infant as long as possible, or telling an adolescent to stay in his teens indefinitely. It is so much better not to "stay" anywhere, but to live each stage of our lives with understanding, vitality, and purpose.

It's All about Attitude

Jerry

Now, fifteen years after my over-the-top fiftieth party, I'm happy to say my perspective on aging has improved dramatically. I've learned that one of the most important components to a successful and fulfilling second half is how we approach it. We can choose to see it as either a new season of life filled with opportunity or as the beginning of the end. It's all about attitude. And it all starts with our thinking. Someone has observed:

Sow a thought, reap a belief.
Sow a belief, reap a habit.
Sow a habit, reap a behavior.
Sow a behavior, reap a lifestyle.
Sow a lifestyle, reap a destiny.

A thought can indeed affect our destiny. The way we think — attitude — has a profound impact on our future.

Paul says in 2 Timothy 4:7, "I have fought a good fight, I have finished the race, I have kept the faith." (NIV) That doesn't sound as if he retired or even slowed his pace in his final years. Greek philosopher Diogenes, when told he should slow down because of his age, mirrored the apostle Paul. He said, "If I were running in the stadium, ought I to slacken my pace when approaching the goal? Ought I not rather to put on speed?" That is a great mindset for the final decades of life. One of the obstacles to a healthy attitude on aging is our society's prevailing negative outlook.

During the colonial period, age was respected, as it is today in other cultures. Early U.S. census data shows that people often claimed to be older than their actual age. Judges and lawyers wore powdered wigs to convey the wisdom believed necessary in the halls of justice. Over the years, that perspective has given way to a lack of respect for the aged and even a dislike for older adults.

What is at the core of this anti-aging outlook? Partly, our society's glorification of youth is to blame. Young people are portrayed as energetic, beautiful, sexy, smart, and competent. It stands to reason then that older people would be perceived as tired, unattractive, sexless, mentally slow, and incompetent. We've all heard the saying: "You can't teach an old dog new tricks," meaning that seniors are not able to learn. Science has proven that platitude wrong.

Dr. Gene Cohen, author of *The Mature Mind: The Positive Power of the Aging Brain*, has conducted major studies on aging. In a *Newsweek* article, he writes that our view of "human development in the second half of life tends to be badly outmoded." He says:

> *We tend to think of aging in purely negative terms, and even experts often define 'successful' aging as the effective management of decay and decline. Rubbish. No one can deny that aging brings challenges and losses. But recent discoveries in neuroscience show that the aging brain is more flexible and adaptable than we previously thought. Studies suggest that the brain's left and right hemispheres become better integrated during middle age, making way for greater creativity. Age also seems to dampen some negative emotions. And a great deal of scientific work has confirmed the 'use it or lose it' adage, showing that the aging brain grows stronger from use and challenge. In short, midlife is a time of new possibility. Growing old can be filled with positive experiences. The challenge is to recognize our potential — and nurture it.*[1]

Why don't we see more evidence of this science reflected in our popular culture?

Dr. Dychtwald points out several myths related to aging. The concepts that older people are in poor health and that older people are unproductive, unattractive, and sexless are untrue.[2] Unfortunately, even though these perceptions of aging are false, many of us have come to believe them and incorporate them into our outlook for the future. Have you ever felt uncomfortable about revealing your age? Are you embarrassed about thinning or graying hair? Do you feel depressed about your age? Begin to ask yourself how you feel and why you feel the way you do when the question of age arises.

Charles and Win Arn point out that at the core of negativity about aging is hopelessness and fear — fear of dying, fear that this life is all there is. They explain, "The self-absorbed baby boom generation, which once proclaimed 'no one over thirty can be trusted,' is a good example. Now well beyond that age, its members often panic at the thought of growing old ..."[3]

If we are to fulfill our prime-of-life potential, we must adjust our attitude about aging. In Romans 12:2, the apostle Paul warns us about conforming to the patterns of the world. We must not allow ourselves to be influenced by the youth-centered atmosphere that surrounds us. With the coming *Age Wave*, these ideas will eventually change, but for now it may take determination, prayer, and an intentional re-focus to have a healthy, godly perspective on aging. My wife has had to come to grips with her own anxieties about aging.

Resisting the Inevitable

Shirley

As Jerry pointed out, aging is an extremely hard pill for us *Baby Boomers* to swallow. Now that we are in mid-life, we resist with a vengeance the idea of growing old. We resent it, we deny it, we try to ignore it, and we secretly fear it. We don't think of ourselves as really aging; certainly we will never be *old*.

It reminds me of a story Jill Briscoe tells about the Sunday morning she fell on the ice as she was leaving church. She actually lost consciousness for a few seconds, and, as she was waking up, she heard the young parking lot attendant speaking to someone on his walkie-talkie. He said, "Quick, I need some help.

An elderly woman has fallen on the ice!" Jill was not only shaken up but astounded. *Wow,* she thought in amazement. *What a bizarre coincidence that another woman would fall at exactly the same time I did!*

More than any other generation, the boomers cling desperately to their departing youth. We join gyms, we have plastic surgery, we buy more cosmetics than anyone in history. Old age is not a season we look forward to or easily accept. But the important message here, no matter what your age, is to enjoy and maximize the stage of life you're in *now.* Until recently, I'm not sure I was doing that.

I am a southerner and proud of it. Born in Mississippi and raised in New Orleans, you can't go any farther south unless you're in a boat. Chicago, our home for the past thirty years, is quite different from the place where I grew up. Chicago is a beautiful and fascinating city, which has given us a rewarding ministry and a great life. However, this southern belle has never adjusted to Chicago's brutal winters.

Even so, there are advantages to living here, like the incredibly beautiful autumn seasons. Down south, the lack of cold weather just doesn't produce the vivid fall colors you find here. I have *finally* come to appreciate and enjoy those first cool, breezy days that eventually bring swirling leaves in every imaginable shade of tan, red, gold, orange, and maroon. I am fortunate to live a few hundred feet from the edge of a forest preserve and look forward to the transformation that takes place every autumn. Though short lived, the panorama of color always leaves me slightly breathless and amazed at the artistic genius of our Creator.

However, it has taken years for me to enjoy the autumn. In the past, as summer came to a close and the leaves began to change, a mild depression and sense of dread set in. *I knew winter was coming!* How could people say this was their favorite time of year when the dead flowers, bitter cold, and icy winds were just around the corner? And the only thing worse than the anticipation of winter is winter itself. Especially when the thermometer drops to single digits and your nose hairs freeze when you step outside!

Frozen fingers and ears, falls on the ice, and snow-packed, slippery streets are not among my favorite things. Anticipating these hardships always brought a sense of dread in the autumn months. But it finally occurred to me I was missing one of the nicest things about Chicago. I was spoiling one lovely season of the year by dreading another. I determined, with God's help, that I would focus on autumn for itself. I would immerse myself in the pleasure of the refreshing cool breezes, the fairyland of falling leaves, and multi-colored trees. I would delight in long walks through the woods, even though I might need a jacket. I would enjoy for a short while the freedom of open windows and no air-conditioning or forced-air heat. I would absorb the uniqueness of the season. And I would *not* dwell on the coming winter.

It's worked. I've gotten better. I can truly say I enjoy the autumn. But it still brings occasional sadness and mixed feelings.

Fallen Leaves and Faded Flowers

A year or so ago in late September, I stepped onto my deck and that familiar bitter-sweet emotion overwhelmed me. There were a few scattered leaves here and there, and my wall of color across the road was coming into its own. My flowers were still blooming, but the petals were definitely fading. The temperature was ideal, the setting sun so much kinder now. It was a perfect day, and I gloried in it. But I had to remind myself to enjoy the moment without dreading the season ahead.

Suddenly, standing there on my deck, I had an epiphany. I believe it was God who impressed upon my heart: *This is where you are in life. You are in the autumn season. Will you miss the beauty of autumn because you are focused on the coming winter?*

Wow! Had I been doing that? I had "celebrated" (yeah, right) my fiftieth birthday a few years before and thought I'd handled that milestone pretty well. But as I searched my heart, I had to admit there was, deep down, a feeling of unrest — a growing sense of dread much like I experienced just before the bitter cold days of winter. Was I letting the fear of growing old spoil what should be the most joyful and fulfilling years of my life? I had to ask myself if I was missing one beautiful season by dreading another. I breathed a prayer that I would *not* let that happen.

I smiled sadly when I realized the scene I was enjoying from my back porch corresponded ironically with my life. The fallen leaves and faded flowers were *me!* Though still fairly attractive for my age, my beauty has certainly faded. A friend once told me that everything on our bodies fades as we age. Our hair, our skin tone, and even our eye color pales slightly, much like my flower petals. The same bearer of good news said our noses get more pointed and our lips get thinner. And like the autumn leaves, everything on the body seems to fall an inch or two. I truly am in the autumn of life, the middle adult years.

My realization led to acceptance and an ongoing attitude change. After all, fallen leaves and faded flowers don't *destroy* the magnificence of autumn. They are *part* of it. I am learning to find the beauty in this stage of my life and embrace it. I am determined, with God's help, to focus on the positive aspects, and not the negative, of where I am right now. A change in my attitude and perspective had helped me appreciate the fall season in Chicago. Likewise, a change in my attitude about aging would be the most important paradigm shift of my life. I have come to see that the final decades of my life need not be the dreaded *winter* of my life. With God's help, I plan to enjoy each season to the fullest, stay as healthy as I can, and embrace the changes that will inevitably come. I will do my best to wring every drop of joy and fruitfulness from my autumn years and not worry about the unknowns of the future. One of my goals for this book is to help you do the same.

Are you anxious about the future? Are you letting a nagging sense of dread about aging ruin your lovely autumn season? You may be facing the reality of your own mortality for the first time and questioning the purpose of your life. Have you made a difference? Is it too late? Have you seen the dreams of your youth fulfilled? Perhaps your life has been more than you could ever have dreamed or imagined, or it may be littered with disappointments. You may worry about possible failing health, financial needs, or losing loved ones. Though our futures are not guaranteed, one thing is sure: *we can trust God.* Isaiah 46:4 says, "I will be your God through all your lifetime, yes, even when your hair is white with age. I made you and I will care for you. I will carry you along and be your savior." (TLB)

When God Dances on Your Potato Chips

Someone emailed me a story of a woman I can identify with very well. She was having a horrific day. She was feeling pressure from a writing deadline, company was due to arrive in a couple of days, and the toilet was clogged. She stopped by the grocery store to pick up a few things, but the long lines were appalling. She arrived home sweaty and frazzled and knew she had to get something on the table for dinner — quick.

She decided on canned cream of mushroom soup, but then remembered she had not bought milk. She set the can aside and went to plan B — leftover baked beans. She lifted the cover and groaned. Even her agreeable husband would not eat beans that looked like green caterpillars. She finally decided on an old standby, hot dogs and potato chips.

She grabbed a new bag of chips from the pantry and gave the bag a pull. It wouldn't come open, so she jerked harder. Still nothing. She took a deep breath and pulled with all her might. With a loud pop the cellophane gave way, ripping wide from top to bottom. The chips flew sky high, all over the kitchen, and she was left holding the empty bag. With a blood curdling scream she yelled, "I can't take it anymore."

The poor woman's husband heard the cry and ran to the kitchen. He just stood there taking in the open soup can, the moldy beans, and one quivering wife standing ankle deep in potato chips. He did the most helpful thing he could think of. He took a flying leap and landed flat-footed on the pile of chips. Then he began to stomp and dance and twirl, grinding the chips into the linoleum.

The astounded woman stared and fumed, but pretty soon had to stifle a smile.

Soon she had joined him in his potato chip dance. She realized she didn't need a clean-up crew as much as she needed an attitude adjustment. That's just what the laughter provided. It wasn't the solution she would have chosen, but it was exactly what she needed. She merely needed a change in attitude.

Has God ever danced on your potato chips? Life often hands us frustrations, challenges, and sometimes tragedy. We cry out to God, hoping He will show up with a celestial broom to clean up our mess. But occasionally He dances on our chips, answering our prayers in ways we never expected. Can we adjust our attitude to embrace what God is doing with our lives?

The most important lesson I have learned in my fifty plus years is that God loves me and He *can* be trusted. Even when the chips are down.

Jerry

A wonderful example of a radical attitude change that led to significant living is a gentleman who accompanied us on one of our many tours to Israel. Jake's wife had passed away about a year prior, and he decided his life, too, was over. He had no plan or purpose, and his future seemed grim. Somehow, his loving daughter convinced the uncooperative Jake to join her on the tour. To say that Jake was a challenge is to put it mildly. He was offensive, complained constantly, and even harassed others on the tour. Finally, after he offended our Jewish driver, we had to threaten to send him home.

Toward the end of the tour, Jake seemed to soften a bit. At the farewell banquet, when Jake stood to share what the tour had meant to him, we collectively held our breath. Through tears Jake said, "I never wanted to go on this tour. My wife died, and I saw no further reason for living. I sat down to die. My daughter made me come on this trip. I have been impossible to get along with, and yet people have kept being nice to me. People have accepted me in spite of the way I've acted. This tour has helped me see that there's life ahead.

I really do have something I can offer, something I can give back."

Jake's story doesn't end with that tour. He stepped out and began touring regularly. He was usually accompanied by a cadre of female seniors. He eventually hooked up with a renowned archeologist and began supporting digs in the Holy Land. Once his attitude changed, Jake plunged headlong into significant living.

Regardless of how you view the first part of life, it's never too late to relinquish your remaining years to Jesus Christ. He knows what is best and can redeem those years in ways you cannot even imagine. Whether you have just entered middlessence or if you are entering the final season of your life, you can grow in significance and purpose. With the Lord's help and guidance, the final years can be fantastic — in fact, they can be pure gold.

The Golden Years

Shirley

What is your attitude about the final season of life? If autumn is the mddle years, then winter must be the final years. But I know I can trust God with the future, whatever it may bring. Perhaps the golden years are named "golden" because they will prove to be the best season of all.

Former Israeli Prime Minister Golda Meir once said, "Being seventy is not a sin." Aren't you glad God doesn't put his children out to pasture when they turn sixty-five or seventy or seventy-five? Our society worships youth, but God values and uses us for His purposes regardless of our age. Noah was six hundred years old when he built the ark! Moses was eighty when he led the children of Israel out of Egypt. The final decades of our lives can be our most productive time if we remain open to the possibilities.

My pastor's wife, Marie Frost, is truly an amazing woman. She is well into her eighties and not even thinking of slowing down. She and her husband Eugene have pastored the First Baptist Church of Big Rock, Illinois, for many years. Though Pastor Eugene has slowed down a bit, he still blesses his congregation with deeply meaningful sermons full of rich Biblical insight and deep theological truths. But Marie is and has always been the driving force in their team.

With untiring energy, she calls the parishioners who are absent and constantly invites new people to church. She runs the Sunday School department with enthusiasm, trains young teachers, and writes and directs the Easter and Christmas programs for the children. She is a well-published author and talented writer who is currently creating Sunday School curriculum for major publishing houses. She is an attractive strawberry blonde who reveals only the occasional gray hair and sports a gorgeous wardrobe any of us could envy. Feisty and opinionated, she is the "youngest" octogenarian I know — an inspiring role model.

I recently mentioned to Marie that I was writing a book on aging. She gave me one of her "looks" as if to say *what would you know about it?* She then informed me she had written a book on aging twenty years ago. It was called *Making the Most of the Golden Years.* "It wasn't any good, though," Marie quipped. "I was too young and had no idea what I was talking about."

Has the autumn season caught you off guard and unprepared? Have you suddenly found yourself in the winter season and feel shell-shocked? Are you running from it, or letting it sadden you, or denying the reality of it. Don't! Let's embrace it and enjoy it. It only takes a change in attitude. Pause for a moment, and ask yourself some questions about your current attitude and outlook on age.

1. Am I ashamed of my age?
2. Has my opinion of myself diminished as I've gotten older?
3. Do I have a nagging sense of dread about aging?
4. Do I fear the future?

Let's begin to practice a positive attitude and root out those negative, stereotypical ideas that plague us. Let's begin to walk the rest of our journey with humor and with joy, and let's search for the matchless beauty of this unique season of life. Come on; let's go. But you'd better grab a jacket. Autumn has arrived.

Action Steps for a Better Attitude:

* *Be honest about how you view aging. Do you consider yourself in the autumn of life — the middle adult years — or the winter season — the senior years? Are you comfortable with where you are?*
* *If you have a negative attitude, read the following scriptures and make a note of the positive promises: Psalms 23, 37, 48, 71, 90, 92, and 103; Proverbs 3:2, 9:11, 10:27, and 16:31.*
* *Make two lists. On the first list, write down all the things you've lost with age (for example, stamina). Now on the second list, write down all the things you've gained with age (for example, grandchildren).*
* *Write out your own definition of successful aging, and make that your mission's statement for the second half of life.*
* *Say a prayer of thanks for the blessings of aging, and ask God to give you a more positive attitude and a spirit of gratitude.*

Suggested Reading

Suggested Reading

Half Time, Bob Buford
Positive Attitudes for the 50+ Years, Willard A. Schofield
A Resilient Life, Gordon MacDonald
What We've Learned So Far, Lucinda Secrest McDowell
Fabulous After 50, Shirley Mitchell with Jane Rubietta

Truths to Guide the Soul

Be fishers of men. You catch them – He'll clean them.

Coincidence is when God chooses to remain anonymous.

Don't put a question mark where God puts a period.

Don't wait for six strong men to take you to church.

Forbidden fruits create many jams.

God doesn't always call the qualified; He qualifies the called.

God promises a safe landing, not a calm passage.

He who angers you controls you.

If God is your co-pilot – swap seats!

Most people want to serve God, but only in an advisory capacity.

The task ahead of us is never as great as the Power behind us.

The will of God will never take you where the grace of God won't protect you.

We don't change God's message; His message changes us.

Give God what is right – not what is left.

A lot of kneeling will keep you in good standing.

Are you wrinkled with burden? Come to church for a faith lift.

The church is prayer-conditioned.

When God ordains, He sustains.

WARNING: Exposure to the Son may prevent burning.

Plan ahead – it wasn't raining when Noah built the ark.

Suffering from truth decay? Brush up on your Bible.

Never give the devil a ride; he will always want to drive.

Nothing ruins the truth like stretching it.

Give Satan an inch, and he'll be the ruler.

Read the Bible – it will scare the Hell out of you.

Second Coordinate:
Spiritual Growth
Growing in Your Relationship with God

We ought always to thank God for you, brothers, and rightly so, because your faith is growing more and more...

2 Thessalonians 1:3 (NIV)

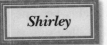

Shirley

Jerry and I attend a very old Baptist church begun by Welsh immigrants about 150 years ago. The small building, over a hundred years old, is an attractive red brick, traditional style. But its most stunning features are the stained glass windows. The leaded work is some of the most magnificent I've seen — surprising on such a modest building. The brilliant colors and symmetry surrounding the sanctuary are a joy to behold. Anyone would notice the lovely windows from the outside, but you cannot truly appreciate their beauty unless you are sitting inside on a sunny morning. The bright light shining through the intricate designs shows off the artistry in all its glory. And the windows have only grown more beautiful with age. Stained glass, regardless of its age, is at its best when the sun shines through.

I see an interesting analogy between those windows and our spiritual lives. We are at our best when the "Son" shines through, and the beauty of a life lived in Christ should only improve with age. However, it is surprising to find how many middle-aged and older adults have never developed a meaningful, personal relationship with Christ. Many who were once enthusiastic about the things of God have grown complacent, spiritually tired, jaded, and even cynical.

Research shows that many older boomers got involved in church for the sake of their kids. They wanted them to have a spiritual foundation. Now that they are empty nesters, they have dropped out of church and moved on to pursue other interests. There is even a diminished interest in church among older adults.

One pastor in Florida has observed a spiritual retirement mentality among his congregation. He says it's difficult to get many retirees involved in volunteer work because they feel they have not only retired from the work force, but also from church work. They think *I've been there, done that*. Spiritually they are coasting and feel it's now the responsibility of the younger church members to carry out vital ministry and service.

You would think as boomers and seniors grow older, when mortality becomes a greater consideration, their thoughts would turn to God and the afterlife. But research does not affirm such thoughts. Not only do older church goers often become complacent about their faith, but the over-fifty community also is not coming to Christ in the numbers you would expect. Why is this? Contrary to what you might think, older Americans are not hardened or resistant to the gospel.

One reason for this disturbing trend could be that the church at large does not have an effective evangelism strategy for this age group. The church's outreach and emphasis have traditionally focused on youth and young adults. Eight in ten churches have a youth director, while only one in forty-nine churches has a senior adult pastor or director.[1]

I have observed this youth emphasis as Jerry and I have visited other churches. It is very apparent in the music, for instance. It seems the music and worship portion of many services is designed exclusively for youth with little sensitivity to the older members of the congregation. As I have looked around, I've noticed that a large percentage of the people fifty and older don't enter into the music and worship. Frequently, the songs are new and difficult to follow. The music seems mostly geared to those who prefer "rock music."

Another reason older adults aren't active participants in church could be that most senior adult programs do not offer enough diversity to appeal to the widely differing interests of the over fifty or sixty age groups. These folks are not one homogenous group, but have very different lifestyles, habits, concerns, hobbies, and needs. You will often hear mature adults say they just don't fit in with "that group of old people."[2] (I feel exactly the same way.) Our churches have their work cut out for them if they are to rise to the challenge of effectively ministering to millions of aging Americans, the dominant population group, in such need of a relationship with God. This outreach gap is the reason Significant Living has joined forces with the Christian Association of Senior Adults (CASA).

CASA is an organization that was begun in 1983 by three southern California churches to provide fellowship and inspiration for their senior adults. Today,

CASA provides resources for church leadership in thirty-six states and Canada, representing a cross-section of denominations and other organizations serving the Boomer and Builder (parents of the boomers) generations. One thing you can do to help your church improve its skill in working with second halfers is by introducing your pastor and church leaders to CASA[3] (www.gocasa.org).

At this strategic point in life, older adults will go one of two ways. They will either grow spiritually, or their relationship with Christ will diminish. Based on ministry to hundreds of seniors, John Thill has broken down this list of choices and the devastating results of having the wrong mindset.

1. *A second halfer will either learn to trust God, or turn to new worthless idols and be overcome with life.*
2. *A second halfer will either become more sensitive to the wind of the Holy Spirit, or will become so brittle that life will be a constant attack.*
3. *A second halfer will either grow in influence and respect, or will increasingly become isolated and marginal.*
4. *A second halfer will either find greater joy and purpose in living dependently on the Lord, or will become increasingly frustrated and depressed because "control" is exposed as the imposter it is.*
5. *A second halfer will learn to understand the jar of clay in which God has placed the treasure of His Spirit, or will live in denial or regret over the consequences of physical aging.*
6. *A second halfer will learn to enjoy solitude as a means to greater fellowship with God, or will become overcome with loneliness or desperately grasp for others with the result of driving them away.[4]*

These are sobering realities to consider as we evaluate our level of maturity in Christ. The dramatic decline in conversions among older adults, along with spiritual complacency, is a real concern to me. At the heart of a truly significant life is a relationship with Jesus Christ. The best way to attain significance is through obedience to Christ and fulfilling His purpose for your life. If you find yourself in midlife or older and have never had a close connection to God, or if you have turned down the burner on your faith over the years, it's never too late to begin or rekindle that relationship.

We are not talking about being religious here. Religion and a relationship with God are practically opposites. Jesus constantly confronted and exposed the religious leaders of His day. He made a point of hanging out with known sinners and tax collectors in addition to the religious elite. He challenged people's thinking; He met physical needs. And He looked at men's hearts, not just their good works. He ultimately gave His life to save the world He loved so much — even though none of us deserve that love. Relationship with God is foundational to this second life coordinate, spiritual growth.

Unconditional Love

Jerry

If you look at a relationship with God from the bottom up, you will find that it's based squarely on the idea of unconditional love. One day when our daughter Vanessa was just three, she climbed into my lap and, with that cherubic smile that is her exclusive property, she melted me with a soft, "Daddy, I love you."

I savored the words for a moment, then I smiled and said, "I love you, too." Vanessa wasn't finished. She was going through her "Why?" stage. So she tilted her head and asked, "Why?" I almost responded too quickly with a standard answer like "Because you're my daughter," or "Because you're so nice." But suddenly I realized that was not the answer I should give. As I contemplated my answer, Vanessa grew impatient. "Why, Daddy?" she demanded. "Why?"

"I don't have a reason, Vanessa," I finally responded. "I just love you. In fact, I love you when you're good and I love you when you're bad." I could tell by the look in her eyes she didn't buy that. "No, you don't," she corrected. "You don't love me when I'm bad."

That startled me a little. Had my actions made her think my love for her was that fickle? Or was her doubt instinctive? Do we humans simply believe that a force as positive as love is reserved for good people?

"Vanessa," I said, "it *is* true. I just love you. And I can't stop loving you." It took her a moment to absorb the new concept. But then she smiled, threw herself against me, and hugged me with all her might. From that time on, we played this little game together, over and over. We both loved it. I called it our affirmation of love.

That incident with Vanessa helped me understand something I should have known all along: God's love for me is not fickle. It is consistent. It's immeasurable and without end. He is the essence of love. The Bible says, "God is love." He cannot help but love us. We may not deserve it. We may scorn it. But it never changes.

Human love can be unstable. It's loaded with conditions. A young couple marries with a love based on unspoken conditions:

> *If you treat me right...*
> *If you are faithful to me...*
> *If you are successful...*
> *If you stay attractive...*

In other words, if you live up to all my expectations — then I will love you. Romans 5:8 says, "But God demonstrates His own love toward us, in that while we were still sinners, Christ died for us."

There are no requirements or conditions for God to love us. And there is nothing we can do to cause God to love us any more or any less than He does. This should free us from the anxiety of conditional love — because when you fail, God doesn't stop loving you. We've all sinned and made mistakes. Whether you're thirty-five or ninety-five or somewhere in between, it's never too late for a new beginning. Merely ask forgiveness and restore the fellowship. That's the beauty of unconditional love!

Take a moment and reflect on whether you really believe, deep down, that God loves you no matter what you've done. When bad things happen, what's your attitude toward God? When things don't go your way, what do you think of God's attitude toward you? If these questions cause you to struggle, spend some time in prayer about experiencing God's love. You might also consult your pastor or a local minister to discuss your feelings.

A Holy Terror

In order to grasp our relationship with God, it's important that we understand who we are in God's eyes. An example from my youth has helped me to understand God's love and its role as a foundation for faith. In spite of my mother's patient and godly input, it took a while for me to embrace her kind of faith. As a kid, I had a lot of insecurities. My family was poor. I was skinny and had buck-teeth so prominent that many of the kids made fun of me. I hung around with kids like me, insecure and looking for attention through negative behavior. I was a "holy terror." If there was a fight in the classroom, I would be in the middle of it. Trouble followed me around like an ugly, loyal mutt.

I had an early-morning paper route, and my fellow paperboys and I often took time off from our routes to sneak over the fence of the local swimming pool for a quick against-the-rules swim. Then we'd hit the local pharmacy and steal pastries the delivery man had dropped off. Eventually the pharmacy owner figured out who had been pilfering the pastries.

He caught up with me as I finished my deliveries and confronted me with the charges. Figuring I was caught, I confessed. "I've asked the police to keep an eye on you," he said, "and I intend to tell your parents."

That was the worst news. If he told my dad about my stealing, the story of my life would be a short story indeed. My father was an honest man; the word stealing was not in his vocabulary. He was also a big man, with huge hands and a long belt. I thought of running away, but I was too young for the Foreign Legion, so I decided I would have to face the consequences.

The phone rang as I walked through the kitchen door, and I knew it was too late. Dad picked up the receiver, and his face changed colors. "Jerry was caught stealing," he told my mother after he had hung up. Mom looked at me, her eyes wide and sad, then turned back to the dishes in the sink. My grandmother, who was sitting at the table knitting, glanced up with a pained expression. I felt like I had been kicked in the stomach. How bad could it get?

I held my breath. My father straightened and walked toward me, his bulky form looking bigger than I ever remembered it. I stepped back. He raised his hand. I cringed. But instead of coming down on me, his hand moved up to cover his face. He sank into the chair behind him.

"Why?" he groaned. "A Rose doesn't steal." Then he mumbled, "My own son," as if the words were making him sick. I gulped down the lump in my throat and looked up at Mom. She wiped her hands on the dish towel and sat down on the arm of Dad's chair.

"I reckon it was a childish prank, honey," she said gently. "We brought Jerry up better than that." Her gray eyes sparked a warning shot at me as she added, "And I suspect he'll never do it again."

"N-n-no, ma'am," I stammered. Mom's words and the pain written on both my parents' faces hurt more deeply than Dad's belt ever could have. In that moment, I vowed to change. I would go straight. I was still only a young boy, but something profound hit home with me in that emotion-charged scene. I learned the hard way that my parents loved me, even when I failed them. But I realized their unfailing love was not cheap or easy. It cost them. My eyes were opened to the value they placed on me. And as I realized my worth, I felt more secure. I could trust their love — which meant I had less need to gain attention through negative behavior.

I still got into trouble occasionally during the next few years, but something had changed. My renewed trust in my parents' love made me feel more worthy and valuable. Their example would gradually help me understand how deeply my Heavenly Father loved me. His acceptance of me was like bedrock — unshakable, unchanging. On the basis of how God sees each of us, we can enter into relationship with Him. Spiritual growth continues as we learn to understand and experience faith.

Three Characteristics of Faith

It took another Rose, not a member of our family, to lead me to a firm commitment to God. His name was Harry Rose, and he led me, kicking and screaming, to the Lord. Harry was a young, enthusiastic minister who came to our church when I was barely fifteen years old. I came to church with a chip on my shoulder, but Harry accepted both me and the chip and treated me as a friend.

When Harry talked about Jesus, his eyes lit up. One Sunday evening, he got my attention. He said, "No matter what you've done, Jesus loves you." I was riveted. I had done plenty. When he talked about God's love and our ability to choose, I realized he was talking about me! As Harry gave an invitation, my heart pulled me to my feet with an overwhelming desire for Jesus. All my years of rebellious, stubborn arrogance dissolved as I felt the love of Jesus pour over me and His forgiveness cleanse me. I had discovered the first and most fundamental kind of faith — *bedrock faith*.

You cannot grow until you are born — your spiritual beginning. Every person's journey of faith begins with a decision to trust Christ's forgiveness. At that point, if we remain in relationship, we can begin to grow.

I began my journey that day under Harry Rose's ministry. I had lowered the pylons of my life all the way to the bedrock. Now my resolve to be "better" would no longer be the flimsy resolve of a guilt-ridden little boy, but a changed heart and life. Sure I have made mistakes and disappointed the Lord many times. But from that moment, I was a new person and have walked hand in hand with the Lord, standing firm on the character of Almighty God — *bedrock faith*.

Through the years, I have never forgotten the foundation on which my life is built.

Bedrock faith, however, is only one dimension of faith. If we are to be spiritually mature, we must understand the three distinct characteristics of faith and exercise them in our lives. All three dimensions of faith are vital to a successful Christian life and meaningful spiritual growth:

- *Bedrock faith – where faith begins and upon which our relationship with God is built;*
- *Inspirational faith – where the thrill, excitement, and motivation leads us to obey God;*
- *Survival faith – combat zone where great battles are fought and great victories are won.*

When God called Shirley and me to Chicago, to step out in faith and plunge into the unknown, that was *inspirational faith*. Many times when the going got rough, I would remember the clear, unmistakable voice of God guiding me. I knew God would see me through any challenge because I had been motivated to obey God through inspirational faith. When I battled cancer in my body, and other times when the way was dark, I clung to my *survival faith*. I claimed the promises of God. I consumed His Word, and my survival faith brought me through to victory and peace. You can find a more in-depth teaching on the three kinds of faith in my book *Deep Faith for Dark Valleys* (Thomas Nelson Publishers).

Intimately linked together, these three pillars become the bridge that supports the Christian's faith walk and healthy growth. These pillars become more important the older you get. Unfortunately, many people entering the second half of life are not even aware of the amazing benefits and blessings God offers us when we put our faith in Him. So when they experience personal struggles or face the new stresses of aging, they become depressed or fearful or collapse under the pressure.

Some older Christians who found God in their youth and have a deep desire to follow Him, have simply gotten off track. Instead of becoming mature spiritually and in a position to mentor and train others in the faith, they struggle to maintain their equilibrium. Wherever you are in your faith walk, it is crucial that your future include solid spiritual growth. It is essential for finding true significance.

Plowing a Straight Course

I heard a story of a farmer who took his son to the fields to teach him to plow. "The secret to plowing a straight row is to pick a fixed object and focus on driving towards it," the farmer explained. He told his son to give it a try, and he would be back in an hour to see how he was doing. When the farmer returned, he was surprised to see wavy, crooked rows. When he asked for an explanation, the son replied, "Well, I did what you told me, but the stump I chose as my fixed object turned out to be a groundhog."

Many get tripped up because they focus on the groundhogs of life. Spiritual growth can come only when we know the difference between the unmovable, unshakeable anchor of God's truth and the world's unstable attractions, such as possessions, power, or financial security. Many Americans may have bigger homes, stock portfolios, and luxury cars, but, for the most part, they are not really happy. Those are not fixed objects; they are groundhogs.

W. Michael Cox, author of *Myths of the Rich and Poor* wrote in *Time Magazine* a few years ago:

> *We are no happier than we were when our incomes were one third of what they are today back in 1948. In fact, our society is experiencing a rising tide of clinical depression, increasing distrust of other people and institutions, and erosion of ties to family, friends, and community.*

Our bedrock is Christ and achieving His purpose. That purpose is different for each of us, but as Paul points out, we must not lose sight of the goal.

Not that I have already attained, or am already perfected; but I press on, that I may lay hold of that for which Christ Jesus has also laid hold of me. Brethren, I do not count myself to have apprehended; but one thing I do, forgetting those things which are behind and reaching forward to those things which are ahead, I press toward the goal for the prize of the upward call of God in Christ Jesus. (Philippians 3:12-14)

Paul certainly does not sound as if he is slowing down in his pursuit of spiritual growth. He uses some interesting phrases in this passage. He says:

- *He has not yet attained.* As we age, we must be careful not to become satisfied with our spiritual life. We cannot afford to adopt the vacation mentality. We must remain students of God's Word and sensitive to the Holy Spirit. The most precious lessons and spiritual insight may well come in our latter years.
- *He is not perfected.* We must all remain teachable and humble. Maturity sometimes brings overconfidence, pride, or a know-it-all mentality. Edmund Burke said, "The arrogance of age must submit to be taught by youth."
- *He presses on toward the goal.* Paul has not slackened his pace. He keeps his goal clearly in view. We must guard against complacency and the temptation to slow down or maintain the status quo. Our level of effort and enthusiasm should be maintained or even increased the older we get.
- *Forgetting those things that are behind.* Guard against spending too much time reliving the "good old days" and glorying in past achievements. On the other hand, don't allow a history of failures or difficulties to limit your possibilities for the future.
- *He reaches forward to those things that are ahead.* I picture Paul striving and grasping for all the wonderful things God has in store for him. He

never forgets where he is headed and the importance of his calling.

How are you doing in the second half? Are you pressing on? Has your spiritual intensity diminished? It's a good idea to examine ourselves occasionally or even ask those around us what they think about our spiritual growth. There are pitfalls lurking in the second half of life. Not only can we become lethargic in our spiritual life, but we sometimes succumb to a false sense of security.

Hardening of the Categories

We all know that hardening of the arteries leads to health crisis and sometimes death. In like manner, "hardening of the categories" in our lives often leads to difficulties and spiritual death. Our patterns of thinking, our habits, and our behaviors can become so hard and inflexible that we are unaware of the dangers. Some people have spent so much time in church attendance, Bible study, and prayer meetings that they have lost their delight in knowing the Lord. The routine has hardened into a category of conduct that leads to rigid legalism instead of vibrant relationship.

It is an important spiritual discipline to work at remaining flexible so we can bend with changing technology, changing attitudes, and changing circumstances. These hardened categories can fool us into complacency and make us vulnerable.

Gordon MacDonald, author of *Ordering your Private World,* former pastor and past president of InterVarsity Christian Fellowship, publicly announced an adulterous affair that nearly destroyed his ministry and family. One of the lessons he learned was "an unguarded strength is a double weakness." In other words, we get so confident about our "strengths" that we let down our guard in certain areas. Mr. MacDonald had for years declared that having an affair or other moral failure was just not in the cards for him. He felt such strong conviction about such conduct that he just knew he would never be tempted. But he was wrong. At a weak moment, when his guard was down because of his over-confidence, he betrayed his marriage, his beliefs, and his ministry. Fortunately, he was able to save his marriage; he went through restoration and continues in ministry today.

As we age, we can be more vulnerable to temptation. More leisure, increased assets, and hidden desires can lead to secrecy and isolation that often lead to a downfall. Vigilance in our spiritual walk is never more important than when we move into the second half of life.

More accidents and deaths occur during the *descent* of Mt. Everest than in the difficult climb to the top. It's when we let down our guard that we give opportunity for the enemy to bring destruction. An unguarded strength is a double weakness, and none of us are immune to the danger. Many lives that crash and burn have succumbed to the hardening of the categories. Flexibility and compassion can get lost in the repetition of habit and routine. Evaluate where you are spiritually, and keep a sensitive spirit to the Holy Spirit's warnings.

Shirley

I like this simple quiz, or checklist, that our friend John Thill created for members of Significant Living. He uses the scriptures to contrast various "character habits" of the over fifty generations. If you answer these questions correctly, it is a good indication that you are spiritually mature. See what these seven questions reveal about your spiritual growth report card.

Pop Quiz for Second Halfers

1. *Are you an affirmer rather than a critic?* Would those around you consider you an encourager, a person who increases your confidence in the Lord, or one who is critical and judgmental? Are you a fault-finder, self-centered, and negative, or a person who builds others up, helps them with their weaknesses, and is appreciative of others' lives and ministries? (Ephesians 4:29) "Do not let any unwholesome talk come out of your mouths, but only what is helpful for building others up according to their needs, that it may benefit those who listen

2. *Are you content rather than a complainer?* Have you learned the secret of being content in every circumstance? Or is your life characterized by complaint? We must learn the habit of thankfulness and gratitude. Paul says that he has learned how to be content whatever the circumstances. (1 Timothy 6:6-8) "But godliness with contentment is great gain. For we brought nothing into the world, and we can take nothing out of it. But if we have food and clothing, we will be content with that."

3. *Are you patient rather than impatient?* Life is more than perfection, deadlines, and accumulation. Do you find that you always need to be first, right, and in control? In our "instant gratification" culture, we miss the joy of giving the gift of time to the Lord and living in His presence. We fret over so much. Patience is actually part of the classic definition of love in 1 Corinthians 13. (1 Corinthians 13:4) (NIV) "Love is very patient and kind …"

4. *Are you a life-giver rather than a taker?* Do you ever struggle with "entitlement?" That's the feeling of being owed something — by the government, the church, one's children, one's friends. The person in whom God dwells has an inexhaustible source of everything he needs for life and godliness. Significant lives are all about giving. (2 Corinthians 9:8) (NIV) "And God is able to make all grace abound to you, so that in all things at all times, having all that you need, you will abound in every good work."

5. *Are you an enlarger rather than a diminisher?* How completely do you see life from God's point of view? Do you help people see the hand and purpose of God in the swirl of events? Do you live in the joy and love of the Lord and help others to do so? Do you have a sense of life's mission and help others to find theirs? (Psalm 112: 4–6) (NIV) "Even in darkness light dawns for the upright, for the gracious and compassionate and righteous man. Good will come to him who is generous and lends freely,

who conducts his affairs with justice. Surely he will never be shaken. A righteous man will be remembered forever."

6. ***Are you a forgiver rather than bitter or unforgiving?*** Do you take offense at what others say? Are you easily offended? When you offend others, are you sensitive to that and quickly seek forgiveness? God's Word is full of warnings about unforgiveness and anger. That is because being a forgiver is so essential to our health and productivity. (Colossians 3: 12-13) (NIV) "Therefore, as God's chosen people, holy and dearly loved, clothe yourselves with compassion, kindness, humility, gentleness and patience. Bear with each other and forgive whatever grievances you may have against one another. Forgive as the Lord forgave you."

7. ***Are you peaceful rather than anxious?*** This could be the heart of the whole checklist. Do we have a deep, consistent, abiding sense of the peace of God? It is sad, actually, that anyone would fail to trust God when His promises are so complete. We worry and fret and fear old age when God's Word gives the assurance of His eternal presence and help. (Isaiah 26:3-4) (TLB) "He will keep in perfect peace all those who trust in Him, whose thoughts turn often to the Lord! Trust in the Lord God always, for in the Lord Jehovah is your everlasting strength."

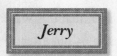

Jerry

We live in a world of chaos and uncertainty. Can you have true peace in the midst of life's challenges? If you can, it's a good indication of your spiritual growth. This truth was illustrated to me in a vivid and most unusual way — by a young bull on the Mexican border.

In the Bull Ring of Life – The Zone of Safety

El Paso is a city that enjoys an ongoing relationship with the people and culture of Mexico. As one who was active in the media and church circles, I made a variety of fascinating acquaintances both in El Paso and across the Rio Grande in Ciudad Juarez. One of the most interesting people I met was a young bullfighter named Fabian Ruiz. At twenty-two years of age, his reputation was growing rapidly.

Through working on a project together at the television station, Fabian and I became good friends. As I grew closer to him and his friends, most of whom were also matadors, they gave me a friendly challenge: I should train with them, they said, and experience the thrill of bullfighting. I was too intrigued to decline.

On many of my weekends, I stood in the sun and sand at the Plaza Monumental, the huge bull ring in Juarez, learning the movements and techniques of the matador — the passes, the use of the cape, the danger signs, and to think like the bull. At night I practiced at home. Jeff, our two-year-old, was the bull. Shirley quickly got tired of this drill. But the practice paid off. Soon the matadors scheduled me for a *tienta*, the event where the young bulls are tested for bravery. If they showed the killer instinct at this stage, they were sent to the ranch for breeding. I did not point it out to my matador friends, but I knew the *tienta* was going to be a test of my bravery, too.

"You are ready," one of the matadors declared. I was not so sure. And Shirley was even less sure. She thought the idea was dumb. And dangerous. Finally, however, she agreed that I couldn't pass up a unique opportunity like this. How often in life do you get to be a matador? She made it clear, however, that this was a "one time only" deal. She would pray for my protection this once — but after that, I was on my own. She drew the line on coming to watch the fight.

On the big day, I nervously stood behind the barrier, fending off anxiety while Fabian gave me last-minute instructions. "My friend," he said, "there are two most important things to remember. First, when the bull charges, plant yourself and do not move your feet. Fear will try to force you, but do not yield." *Easy for you to say,* I thought. "The bull will charge anything that moves so the cape must be the only thing moving." I nodded dumbly. "Second," he continued, "remember the *querencia*. You must not forget the *querencia.*"

I remembered the word from my training. The *querencia* is the bull's "zone of safety," the area in which the bull feels safe. The moment he is released into the arena, the bull instinctively creates a *querencia*. He thinks that, because the few square yards around him are unthreatening at the moment, they will always be so. From that moment on, the bull will always feel safe within that area and unsafe outside of it. For the matador, the *querencia* is filled with danger. Since it's difficult to get the bull out of his safety zone, the matador is often forced to go in after him. This puts the matador in close proximity to the bull, where he must now operate on the bull's terms.

Once the bull has moved outside the *querencia,* he becomes intensely uneasy and wants to return immediately to his space. In fact, he will go charging for his zone of safety and literally run through anything that gets in his way. The matador must not get between the bull and the *querencia.* Many young bullfighters have ended up on the bull's horns simply by getting in his path as he ran for safety.

With sweat beading on my upper lip, I stepped into the arena. I wish I could report that I was brilliant — a natural. But it was not meant to be. At the end of my first and only bull fight, I had left a strip of flesh from the side of my knee on the young bull's horns. I immediately retired from my career as a matador.

The encounter left me with a bruised ego and a profound lesson which has stuck with me. The *querencia* is only an illusion. There is no safety zone for the bull. Sooner or later, his blood will stain the sand of the Plaza Monumental.

People have *querencias,* too. They feel if they can be financially secure, then they will be safe. But the stock market fails, and they watch their comfortable retirement go up in smoke.

A young man dreams of becoming a great civic leader. He imagines he will gain respect and power and that such a life will make him happy. As his career advances, he keeps his eye on that goal and belligerently charges anything that comes between him and success. But even if he gets there, he finds the *querencia* has not protected him from a failed marriage, estranged children, loneliness, and misery.

We have all heard of famous, successful people who have ended their lives in suicide. Some of the world's greatest performers, most brilliant minds, and biggest stars have crashed and burned through drug use, dangerous lifestyles, and self-destructive behavior. Because when they reach the top, they find only emptiness and disappointment. Just like the bull, they find out too late the truth about the *querencia*.

Spiritual Discipline

I wish I could say that spiritual growth automatically comes with age. But that doesn't happen. It takes spiritual discipline and hard work. This doesn't mean we work for our salvation. That is a free gift that stems from God's unconditional love and Jesus' death on Calvary. But *spiritual growth* takes effort. That's the reason many Christians never get past the infant stage. In the next chapter, we will discuss in detail some of the godly habits necessary for significance. But here are a few basic disciplines necessary for spiritual growth:

- Begin your journey of faith by exercising *bedrock faith* and accepting Christ's provision for salvation.
- Maintain your relationship by close communication with God through prayer, worship, and Bible study.
- Practice listening for God's direction and respond to His guidance by exercising *inspirational faith*.
- Be faithful to church attendance and fellowship with like-minded believers, and be willing to serve others sacrificially.
- Live a holy life through obeying the commands of God's Word such as Micah 6:8, Galatians 5:14-26, 1 Corinthians 13, etc.
- Develop godly character traits through putting others before yourself and imitating Jesus's example and other godly role models.
- Keep your faith strong in adversity through exercising *survival faith*.

I want to end this chapter with the best news of all. If we know Christ, we have a genuine *querencia*. We can enter the final decades of life knowing where our true safety zone is. We can have peace in spite of the unknowns of the future.

There is more help for you in the following chapters as we pursue life habits and principals that lead to significance. If you follow these principles, you cannot help but grow your relationship with God. There is beautiful synergy between spiritual growth and significance. My prayer is that you will know Christ in a new and dynamic way.

Don't even think of entering into the second half of life without Him. We don't have to take this road trip alone.

Action Steps for Spiritual Growth:

• *Ask yourself if you understand the concept of God's unconditional love. Can you accept it fully, or do you find yourself trying to earn His love?*

• *Revisit the three kinds of faith: bedrock, inspirational, survival, and see if you can think of examples of all three in your past.*

• *Honestly evaluate whether your religious rituals have resulted in rigid legalism and a false sense of spiritual security. Or have you remained flexible, teachable, and in right relationship with God?*

• *Take the "Pop Quiz for Second Halfers," and think of examples when you have passed and other times you have failed. Ask God how you can grow. Compare your level of spiritual maturity today with your spiritual walk as a young Christian. Has your spiritual intensity increased or diminished?*

Suggested Reading

The Case for Christ, Lee Strobel
Don't Waste your Life, John Piper
When I Don't Desire God, John Piper
Spiritual Seasons, Thomas A. Vaughn
Living the Life You Were Meant to Live, Tom Peterson

A True Story

An elderly Florida lady did her shopping, and upon returning to
her car, found four males in the act of leaving with her vehicle.
She dropped her shopping bags and drew her handgun, proceeding to
scream at the top of her voice, "I have a gun and I know how to use it!
Get out of the car!"

The four men didn't wait for a second invitation. They got out and ran
like mad. The lady, somewhat shaken, proceeded to load her shopping bags
into the back seat of the car and get behind the wheel. She was so shaken,
she couldn't get the key into the ignition. She tried and tried, and then
it dawned on her why. A few minutes later she found her own car
parked four or five spaces farther down.

She immediately drove to the police station. The sergeant to whom she
told her story doubled over with laughter. He pointed to the other end of the
room, where four pale men were reporting a car jacking by a mad, elderly
woman described as white, less than five feet tall, glasses, curly white hair,
and carrying a large handgun.

No charges were filed.

A Woman's Age

The best way to tell a woman's age is when she is not around.

When a woman tells you her age, it's okay to look surprised, but don't scowl.

A man who correctly guesses a woman's age may be smart,
but he's not very bright.

An archaeologist is the best husband any woman could have:
The older she gets, the more interested he is in her.

The only time a woman wishes she were a year older is when she is expecting a baby.

An older woman was born in the year of our Lord only knows.

Her age is her own business, and it looks like she's been in business a long time.

Third Coordinate:
Consistency
Developing Godly Habits

How thankful I am to Christ Jesus our Lord for choosing me as one of His messengers, and giving me the strength to be faithful to Him.

1 Timothy 1:12 (TLB)

Shirley

Have you ever started a new project or activity with enthusiasm, but after a few days or weeks found yourself unmotivated and inconsistent? It reminds me of the man who received a week of exercise at the local health club as a present from his wife. He called and made a reservation with someone named Tonya, a 26-year-old aerobic instructor and athletic clothing model. He was very enthusiastic about his new exercise program. The following is his diary of the week:

Day 1: Started out at 6 a.m. Tough to get up, but worth it. Tonya is a goddess, blonde hair, dazzling white smile. She showed me the treadmill, then took my pulse. It was alarmingly high. Could have been her outfit. Tonya was encouraging as I did my sit-ups, but it was hard to hold my gut in the whole time. This is going to be GREAT!

Day 2: Took a whole pot of coffee to get me out the door, but I made it. Tonya made me lie on my back and hold this heavy bar. Then she put weights on it for heaven's sake! Legs were a little wobbly on the treadmill, but muscles feel GREAT!

Day 3: The only way I can brush my teeth is by laying the toothbrush on the counter and moving my mouth back and forth over it. Driving was okay as long as I didn't have to steer. Tonya was a little impatient with me today; she said my screaming was disturbing the other members.

Day 4: Tonya was waiting for me with her teeth in a full snarl. I can't help it if I was an hour late. It took that long to tie my shoes. She wanted me to lift the dumbbells. Not a chance, Tonya. The word "dumb" must be there for a reason. I hid in the men's room until she sent Lars looking for me.

Day 5: I hate Tonya more than any human being has ever hated anyone in the history of the world. If there were any part of my body not in extreme pain, I would hit her with it. The treadmill flung me back into a Physical Education teacher which hurt like crazy. Why couldn't it have been someone softer like a music teacher?

Day 6: Got Tonya's message on my answering machine, wondering where I am. I lacked the strength to use the TV remote, so I watched 11 straight hours of the Weather Channel. Thank goodness that's over. Maybe next year my wife will give me something more fun like a colon exam or gum surgery!

Well, maybe you've had a little better track record at *your* gym, but all of us struggle with consistency. We have good intentions, but find it much more difficult to follow through and stay committed.

Jerry

Owen Carr was the founder and first president of Channel 38 here in Chicago. Though I don't see Owen very often, I know exactly what he did this morning. He got up very early, around four or five a.m. He showered and dressed, most likely in a suit and tie. Then he read seven pages in his Bible. After that, he got on his knees for his prayer time.

The reason I am so sure that's what he did this morning is because he has gone through that exact routine every day of his life since his youth. This year, he will read his Bible through twice, seven pages a day, marking his favorite passages and making notes in the margins. When he works his way from Genesis to Revelation, he will then give that Bible to one of his grandchildren. (His children have also received marked-up copies of the Bible from their father.) The next day, he will begin at Genesis with a new Bible.

Now in his seventies, he is still actively involved in ministry. I admire Owen's strong faith and what he has accomplished for the Kingdom. But as much as anything, I admire his *consistency*.

Being habitual is not necessarily a positive. It's what we sometimes call "a rut," or a "hardening of the categories," described earlier. My dad was also a very habitual person. He liked things done the same way every time — like mowing the lawn, for instance. Dad always did it exactly the same way, mowing very straight lines from left to right, then right to left. I used to drive my dad crazy when I mowed. I liked to try different things. I might mow my initials in the lawn first — or mow in circles. It was much more interesting, and the grass still got cut just the same. But my dad made it clear as long as I was mowing *his* lawn, it would be mowed *his* way.

Consistency = Commitment to Excellence

I know a couple who recently visited a new church. A lady came over to them and said, "I see you are sitting in my seat." She said it good naturedly, but it was obvious she had gotten into the habit of sitting in exactly the same seat every Sunday. The new couple made a point of sitting in another area next time.

As we age, we sometimes do get in a rut. We might be afraid to try new things or step out of our comfort zone. We could just be too "set in our ways" to be open about new concepts or new ways of doing things. That is not healthy. There is a difference between being habitual and being consistent. Habitual implies merely a routine — doing usual, ordinary things over and over.

There is a world of difference in consistency. Consistency at its best grows out of a noble motivation and high level of character. It can include reliability, steadfastness, dedication, loyalty, and devotion. On the other hand, it's possible to be consistently *bad.* Consistency in the best sense requires *commitment to excellence.* So in this chapter, we will explore developing godly habits in order to develop consistency that leads to excellence in all areas of life.

Achieving Excellence in a Mediocre World

Excellence is a trait that is too often missing in the lives of aging adults. Retirees who spent decades being consistent as an employee, arriving on time, having a high standard in appearance and work ethic, can let down their standards when they retire and settle for mediocrity. Unfortunately, this mentality is reflective of our entire culture. We have all been disappointed at the lack of quality of new products we buy. Appliances and furniture are good examples. We discover that the new washing machine we buy doesn't last nearly as long as our old one. The inner workings are now made of plastic instead of metal. Furniture that used to be hand-carved wood is now molded of plastic and often contains only a thin veneer of wood. No wonder many of us prefer the solid workmanship of antiques.

Health care, which is such a concern to older adults, just isn't what it used to be. With managed health care and rampant malpractice suits against doctors, too often we just don't receive the same quality of care we used to. This is certainly not true for everyone in the medical community, but sometimes it's merely a case of settling for mediocrity over excellence.

Consistency is tied closely to the concept of *commitment*. It's easy to begin a task with enthusiasm and good intentions, but the measure of real commitment is the manner in which we complete the task.

One spring our daughter Vanessa got excited about the idea of planting a garden. We put together a 12-by-6-foot box garden, bought special soil, visited the nursery, and planted tomatoes, carrots, and other vegetables. She was thrilled, enchanted by the whole process.

A month later, I found myself alone, pulling weeds, thinning carrots, watering, and fertilizing "Vanessa's" garden. She was nowhere to be seen. She had, of course, lost the passion. Her inspiration had withered, and the now boring requirements had deflated her enthusiasm. She lacked genuine commitment.

In the Christian walk, you can expect similar experiences, and you can counteract them when you draw on your *inspirational faith*. Remember God's Word to you, and then continue to walk in that Word. In my first six months with the television ministry in Chicago, I had to review my calling frequently to keep from fleeing. Even now I have to revisit my calling occasionally to keep my enthusiasm strong. A young missionary taught me a lesson on renewing the fervency of commitment.

The Red Light District

Many years ago, I walked into the green room (a holding area for guests before going on the air) to meet the guest for my daily television program. My producer had prepped me on the guest. He was a missionary from Holland who worked in the red light district of Amsterdam.

If you've ever been to the Netherlands, you know what a beautiful country it is — quaint, doll-house dwellings with lace curtains, miles and miles of tulips, a roadmap of criss-crossing canals, and colorful country folk complete with wooden shoes. But when you leave the villages and enter Amsterdam, the picture changes dramatically. The city pulsates with people of all descriptions anytime day or night. Like any large city, there are the homeless, the poor, the drug addicts, and the runaway teens. But Amsterdam offers a wide array of unusual characters. I remember one beautiful young girl, dressed like a bride in a dirty, tattered gown, wandering the streets with a glazed stare. The hopelessness and sin are truly heartbreaking.

But the worst part of town is the red light district. Prostitution is legal in Amsterdam. The seedy area consists of row after row of small apartments with a red light outside. Each has a large picture window. And sitting on display are women and girls of all ages. A man can literally window shop until he finds someone who appeals to him. Shirley and I will never forget the despair we felt for those poor women.

When I saw the young man who was to be my guest, all the memories of Amsterdam came rushing back. I was so surprised, I could hardly speak. The missionary had his head practically shaved on one side and spiked on the other. He was wearing the strangest suit I had ever seen with huge shoulder pads and elastic at the ankles of his pants. And he had more than one earring. I am somewhat open to new things, but that was way over the top. A missionary dressed like that was completely unacceptable. I greeted the young man and then went to find my producer.

"What are you doing to me? I asked. "I don't want to interview this man. I don't even want him on my show dressed like that." The producer assured me he had a great testimony and to go ahead with the interview.

Still skeptical, I opened the show by asking, "Working in that kind of environment, how can you not be influenced by those around you?"

The young man said, "That's a good question, and it is very difficult. My wife and I have made a pact. Anytime we can walk the streets and not be deeply moved by the sin and despair we see around us, we leave for two weeks. We fast and pray and ask God to give us fresh eyes to see again the horror of the sin of those He has called us to reach."

I was stunned as I remembered all the times I have walked the streets of Chicago without feeling that kind of concern. I had obviously misjudged the sincere young man. I followed the couple's ministry for several years and watched the outstanding success they had in perhaps one of the most difficult of mission fields.

Perhaps if we find ourselves waning in our commitment to excellence, we should do what the young missionaries did. We should pray earnestly, asking God to renew our vision and keep our spirits sensitive to the opportunities around us.

The uncommitted, uncaring person will be mediocre. The person with the drive to dig in, the character to grapple with a problem until he finds a solution, and the perseverance to stick to the task until it is completed will excel. This commitment is crucial for second halfers because it shapes the final epoch of their lives and produces the critical key of consistency. If they can live out this vital truth, they will surely find significance.

Consistency in Prayer – Pray Without Ceasing

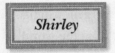

Shirley

Have you ever wondered how anybody can really fulfill the biblical command to "pray without ceasing?" (1 Thessalonians 5:17) This admonition has intimidated many Christians, especially when they think of prayer as a physical posture. But we can get in the habit of praying throughout the day. Prayer should not be only ten or fifteen minutes of morning or evening devotions, although that is a commendable habit. Unceasing prayer means that we live in a spirit of prayer.

Our expressions to God should come as a spontaneous reaction to what is inside us. A volcano erupts because it can no longer contain what is bubbling inside. Likewise, prayer is a release of our innermost feelings about God, about ourselves, and about others. Prayer should contain adoration and praise, thanksgiving, confession of our sins, and supplication — asking God for what we need and asking for the needs of others. We can practice the presence of God where prayer is as natural as breathing. We can move into the realm of spontaneous prayer — the kind that bursts forth anywhere, at any time, from the very depth of our being! Prayer is really about relationship.

Yet many of us who have known God for years tend to slack off on our commitment to prayer. If we're not careful, we adopt the "been there, done that" mentality. The over fifty generation has perhaps the greatest prayer responsibility of any group. Our years of experience, our mellowed wisdom, and our decades of relationship with God make us high-value intercessors. There is a deeper level of prayer, however, that smacks of that word again — commitment — that produces excellence.

Bob Sorge, one of my favorite writers on the subject of personal devotions, tells the story of Chris and DeAnn. They were a young couple who faced a major financial crisis. They decided to spend some time praying together about the situation. As they prayed together, they heard an audible voice say, "If you need help, call 9-1-1." The voice repeated the message four or five times. Thinking it could be coming from the garage, they slowly opened the door and looked inside. Everything seemed in perfect order, except that in the center of the floor lay a toy ambulance. Chris picked it up and pushed a button next to the emergency lights. "If you need help, call 9-1-1." As the couple stood wondering how in the world this mechanism could have activated itself, Chris felt the Holy Spirit say, *If you need help, call 9-1-1 — Psalms 91:1.*

Chris and DeAnn returned to the family room and read the verse together: "He who dwells in the secret place of the most high shall abide under the shadow of the Almighty." They realized God was telling them to renew their commitment to the secret place of prayer, meditation, and relationship with Christ. They knew God would direct them in their financial decisions as they developed intimacy with the Lord.[1] Bob doesn't relate the end of the story, but I have a feeling Chris and DeAnn were just fine.

The *secret place* refers to a special time set aside to talk with God and then listen to what he has to say back to us. These are not quick, multi-tasking prayers while you wash dishes or exercise. I believe the secret place takes *time!* Not necessarily long periods of time, but a deliberate occasion, an appointment, if you will, when our entire focus is on intense communication with the God of the universe. In these special moments, God can give us direction and instruction for the future. He can burden us for ministry or take away worry or fear and give peace. As we spend quality time with the Lord, we begin to actually take on the characteristics of Jesus himself. Then we are ready for Him to gently lead us into areas of significance that we might never have thought of on our own. The *secret place* is where our commitment to excellence is born.

We should enter into the secret place of prayer like a starving person to the banquet table — with a sense of relief, knowing God can meet our every need. And when the need is met, we should thank and praise Him even more. I cannot tell you when to pray — whether in the morning or evening — or how long you should pray. But the important thing is you are *consistent*.

Listening for God's Voice

Unceasing prayer is really an attitude more than an action. It is a mindset focused on God — a listening ear and open heart that waits to receive instruction. But how do we recognize God's voice? There are so many voices clamoring for our attention. There are the voices of friends and family who have our best interests at heart, but don't always know God's will. There is the voice of the secular media and the "spirit of the world" that could get us off track. There is the voice of the enemy of our souls, Satan, who tempts us to follow our own selfish desires. And there is the voice of reason and common sense. Sometimes even that voice seems contrary to what God is saying! How do we know when God is speaking to us?

Jerry

After college, I joined the U.S. Coast Guard reserves. When I completed boot camp, I was assigned to sea duty on board a 311-foot cutter. In my spare time, I enjoyed visiting the radio control center to watch the radioman in action. As he sat in front of a complicated instrument panel, all kinds of "noise" came through the speaker. There were Morse Code beeps, several voices (some in other languages), static, whistles, and cracks. I wondered how he could possibly understand any of the messages being sent through all the noise. But he sat calmly writing down the critically important messages for our ship. I was amazed that he could decipher the right message amidst all the confusing cacophony of sounds. When I asked him how he did it, he smiled and replied confidently, "I have a trained ear."

Christians desperately need to have ears trained to hear God's voice. Today, we're bombarded with messages from every possible direction. But in the midst of all the confusion, we *can* hear God's voice, telling us the course He wants us to take. But it takes practice, and we have to learn to be quiet … and listen. We learn to recognize His voice through consistently spending time in prayer, especially in the secret place of intimacy.

Shirley

We also must be consistent in praying for our unsaved loved ones. When we pray for years and it seems nothing is happening, we tend to get complacent about it. We get weary. In theory we still believe for our loved ones, but our consistency and commitment to pray for them wanes or dies completely.

I did not grow up in a Christian home. I found Christ in a small neighborhood church at eight years of age. From the moment I began my spiritual journey, I prayed that my parents would begin theirs. As a young girl, I would weep and pray fervently for my parents' salvation. But I had to pray that prayer for over forty years! They both came to Christ in the last years of their lives — not the way I would have chosen. But God was faithful.

After my father died, my mother decided to take a tour of Israel with Jerry and me — which was very surprising. When I told Jerry, he became a prophet.

He said, "Your mother is going to accept Christ, and I am going to baptize her in the Jordan River." That is exactly what happened! Standing on the banks of the Jordan River, on her seventy-second birthday, she raised her hand to accept Christ. Then Jerry baptized her in the frigid waters. She was wearing a rented white robe, a hotel shower cap, and a grin from ear to ear. It was a major highlight of my life. All the years of prayer for her, and my dad, were well worth the effort.

Never give up on those loved ones and friends. Be consistent in prayer. Pray not only for their salvation but for their protection, for health and prosperity, for spiritual growth, and for God to strengthen their marriages. Become an intercessor in the last half of your life like never before. It pays big dividends.

Consistency in Bible Study

Jerry

I've been a Christian for fifty years, and God's Word is just as important to me today as it was when I was a brand new Christian. If we are to find God's plan for significance in our lives, we need a roadmap. Yes, we can sense God's voice through urgings and impressions as we pray. God can speak to us through the wise counsel of friends, family, pastors, and others. Some may even experience hearing the audible voice of God. But the most reliable roadmap we have to finding God's will for the rest of our journey is God's Word.

It doesn't matter how many times you've read through the Bible or how many sermons you've heard. God can give you the desired answer from His Word at the very moment you need it. Of course, the Bible has a general message to all of God's people. But it is a mystery how the Bible can be very *specific* and *personal* in pointing you in the right direction in your unique circumstances.

Consistency in studying the Word is critical in the final decades of life because it can give us peace, courage, and victory when we face trials and challenges. In times of illness, loss of loved ones, financial problems, or loneliness, God's Word can build our faith and provide an effective weapon to defeat the enemy.

I'm reminded of a sailing experience I had years ago. A friend called and asked if I would like to join a group of five in sailing a 44-foot sailboat across Lake Michigan. The owner had finished his vacation in Ludington, Michigan, and needed someone to sail the craft back to the yacht harbor at Waukegan, Illinois. Since I'm a sailing enthusiast without a boat, it only took me about two seconds to say, "Yes." Within a few days, I was stowing my gear aboard the sleek racing yacht.

The first day out, we sailed down the lovely western shore of Lower Michigan. Late in the afternoon, we sailed into the harbor in Holland, Michigan, for an overnight stay. As we eased our way into a quiet, tree-lined cove, we put out the anchor. With the anchor in place, we could settle comfortably on the deck, enjoy the warm summer breeze, and tell boat stories. The water lapped lazily against the hull of the yacht. But throughout the night, the anchor held the boat steady. It prevented us from being carried by the current into another boat or from "going aground" on one of the many sandbars around us.

At first light, we grabbed a quick breakfast and prepared to head out once again. We "hauled up anchor" and carefully eased our way out of the narrow cove. It was delicate work. The shallow sandbars on either side of us were difficult to see. We did our best to hold a straight course.

Suddenly, without warning, we stopped short in the water. We had drifted just slightly, and now we were locked tightly in the sand. We held an emergency crew conference and decided the solution was the anchor. We lowered a small, rubber dinghy over the side. Then Tony, our bravest crew member, climbed into the dinghy. We lowered the anchor over the edge, and Tony eased the heavy object into his lap. He gently paddled about sixty yards away from the yacht, holding his grip on the anchor. Slowly the anchor's rope stretched out the full distance between the two crafts. Tony then dropped the anchor over the side of the dinghy and tugged on it a few times to make sure it had dug into the bottom. He signaled us that he was ready.

On our end of the anchor rope was an electric winch. As we reeled in the anchor rope, it moved our boat toward the anchor. Within a moment or two, we were off the sandbar and headed for the lake. We picked up Tony and the dinghy and headed out of the cove to begin the seventy-five-mile run across the lake. It was pure joy.

Thank God for the anchor! Not only did it serve to hold us steady throughout the night, it also pulled us off the sandbar and out of danger.

In our daily lives, the Bible is our anchor. We're living in a swift, ever-changing current of philosophies and fads and social values. A hundred years ago, the moral waters were calmer. In this modern age, we need the anchor of God's Word to hold us steady. Second halfers need the timeless wisdom of God's Word to become spiritually mature and to become the stable role models younger generations so desperately need.

When we are grounded in God's eternal truth, we will not be swayed by the latest pop theology or the post modern mindset. Paul says to the Ephesians. "… we will be mature and full grown in the Lord, measuring up to the full stature of Christ. Then we will no longer be like children, forever changing our minds about what we believe … Instead, we will hold to the truth in love, becoming more and more in every way like Christ." (Ephesians 4:13-15) (TLB)

And remember when the waters are rough, we have an anchor. When we get into trouble — when the floodwaters of tragedy threaten to overwhelm us — it is the anchor of God's Word that rescues us. It is always there, always available to steady our lives.

Consistency in Relationships

Shirley

As we age, we can begin to take our relationships with others for granted, especially the most important one — our spouse. The person who we are supposed to love above all others, except God, often becomes merely a fixture, a habit, even an irritation at times.

French actor Jeanne Moreau said, "Age doesn't protect you from love. But love, to some extent, protects you from age." The perfect depiction of this idea is an older couple who is still so in love they can't seem to keep from touching, teasing, laughing, and having fun together. And regardless of their age, they always seem *young*.

But reality is that romance, respect, and thoughtfulness between newlyweds fade away far too quickly. More than likely, you realized in the first year of marriage that you didn't have as much in common with your spouse as you once believed. The late Erma Bombeck lists the commonalities she and her husband shared before marriage:

> *We both chewed only half a stick of gum and saved the other half.*
> *(How many people did that!) We both ... hated communism, and what*
> *was the other thing? Oh yes, we both loathed going to the dentist.*[2]

And by the time we reach 50, most of us have realized we are *not* going to change our spouse like we had hoped. Erma quickly discovered it was an uphill battle.

> *There had been no progresss ... He still had the burr haircut. He continued*
> *to hang out with ... the guys ... He was a night person and I was a day person ...*
> *He didn't tan... He left his entire wardrobe in his closet regardless of whether*
> *it was winter or summer. How could you live like that with seersuckers and*
> *wools side by side? ... Not only that, I discovered the man was incapable of*
> *putting a toilet seat lid down.*[3]

The longer we are married, the more obvious it becomes that we probably won't change our spouses very much. If our marriage goes the distance, we have to adjust, be flexible, and love unconditionally. We also have to be consistent in the hard work of growing a relationship.

One of the most moving interviews I ever did for my TV program *Aspiring*

Women was with Gracia Burnham. Gracia and her husband Martin were missionaries in the Philippines. They made national headlines when they were kidnapped by an Al Sayyaf terrorist group for ransom.

The world followed their story in horror as the terrorists dragged the Burnhams and other captives through the Philippine jungles for more than a year. They had only the clothes they were wearing, very little food, and were in grave danger. Martin was eventually killed by friendly fire, and Gracia was released.

I asked Gracia to describe her relationship with Martin during those nightmare months in the jungle. She said she came to love and appreciate Martin more than she had during their entire marriage. Everything else had been stripped away. Her children, her clothes, her safety, her make-up — all the trappings that made her who she was to that point — were gone. Everything except Martin.

Gracia said, "After all those years of marriage, I discovered I hadn't really known my husband at all. I watched Martin's character emerge over and over. I saw him reach out to the very enemies who held us captive."

She discovered the man Martin was in the most horrific of circumstances. She was able to continue on in spite of her deep despair because of his strength and encouragement. In fact, Gracia believes she was not sexually molested because the terrorists had so much respect for Martin.

Tell Them Now

Gracia's story inspired me to appreciate aspects of my husband's character that I had come to take for granted. I began to focus on his good points and minimize his faults. I try harder to appreciate him while I still have the opportunity and make an effort to *tell him* daily how I feel about him.

A friend shared with me how his family had played a game during a family gathering. The game was simple, but quickly took on a serious and poignant quality. Each family member chose another as a partner. They had to pretend they were on an airplane that was about to crash. They had ten minutes to write the last words they would ever be able to speak to that person.

At first, everyone moaned and complained about such a morbid "game."

But after much cajoling from my friend, everyone got into the exercise and gave it their best shot.

The results were quite dramatic and emotionally charged. As each one began to read the simple words scribbled hurriedly on their scrap of paper, something extraordinary happened. The atmosphere in the room turned thick with emotion. The person reading became choked up with quivering lips and tear-filled eyes. The one receiving the precious words shed tears, and some even sobbed. Around the room they went, reciting words of love, appreciation, affirmation, and fond memories.

At the end of the exercise, everyone just sat for several minutes in silence. No one wanted to disturb the warmth and richness of the moment. Finally, those who had cried the hardest began to chuckle. The laughter started softly and grew into a riotous outburst of joy. My friend's family learned the power there is in shared words of love. And yet, we race through our days (and lives) without telling those we love exactly how we feel. Get into the habit of verbalizing all that you appreciate about your spouse, family members, and even co-workers. Give affirmation, encouragement, and compliments often. When you consistently work on relationships, you will never find yourself isolated or alone.

Consistency in Church Attendance

When our children were at home, our family was always consistent in church attendance. We were there at least three times a week, and I rarely missed choir rehearsals. Not only were Jerry and I very committed to our church, but we knew it was important to establish a pattern of faithfulness and set a good example for our children.

However, once the kids were gone and it was just the two of us, I found it easier to miss church occasionally. After all, no one was watching, and what harm could it do? But this is a dangerous attitude and a common problem with second halfers. When our calendars are no longer tied up with our children's activities and we transition into other priorities, it's easy to become inconsistent in attending church, Bible studies, or small groups. Paul says in Hebrews 10:

24, 25, "And let us consider one another in order to stir up love and good works, not forsaking the assembling of ourselves together, as *is* the manner of some, but exhorting *one another,* and so much the more as you see the Day approaching."

Why is church attendance so important? As Paul says, it stirs up love, good works, and an opportunity to bless and encourage one another. Perhaps now, more than in any other stage of life, we need the fellowship, connection, and spiritual teaching of regular, consistent church attendance.

Consistency in Giving and Good Works

We have mentioned that true significance usually includes other people. If you have spent your life living only for yourself, it's difficult to suddenly begin the habit of reaching out to others. Being generous with our money is an especially difficult habit to acquire.

Jerry once interviewed an older minister and evangelist on his program. He asked him, "What is the secret to real revival?"

Without hesitation the old gentleman said, "Revival, my friend, starts in the pocketbook."

Slightly offended by this flippant answer, Jerry asked again, "No, seriously, where does revival begin?"

Sticking to his answer, the seasoned preacher explained that if a Christian can come to the point where he is willing to let go of his money, then his heart is ready for genuine spiritual growth. How true!

Sometimes, however, money is the easiest way for us to give. Oswald Chambers said, "When we speak of giving, we nearly always think of money. Money is the lifeblood for most of us. We have a remarkable trick — when we give money, we don't give sympathy; and when we give sympathy, we don't give money."[4]

Giving to God's work and giving to the poor are scriptural directives. (1 Timothy 6:18) Your giving may never receive the notice of others. You may be called simply to be a servant and work behind the scenes. But giving and service can be important keys to opening the door to significance.

Consistency in Work Habits

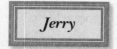

When a person retires, he or she may understandably want to take it easy. They have had years of career-related stress, a demanding schedule, possibly an exhausting commute to work, or a physically demanding job. One of the best parts of the retirement years is the ability to get more rest and have more time for leisure activities and for doing the things you've never had time to do.

However, a real danger in traditional retirement is the temptation to let good work habits slide or disappear. You still need to be consistent in scheduling your day to include not only rest and enjoyable activities, but also some type of work and accomplishment. Occasionally, we all need down time and an opportunity to just relax. But this kind of inactivity over time develops into a destructive habit. With at least half of our lives over; it is essential to spend the last part wisely. Wasted time robs our lives of significance and robs us of personal self-esteem.

Be diligent in good personal work habits. Get up at a reasonable time, shower, and get dressed. Pay attention to personal grooming. Continue to take pride in your appearance — even if your day will be spent alone. It will make you feel better about yourself.

Many retirees are finding that the leisure activities they anticipated just aren't that satisfying. Dr. Dychtwald notes that the suicide rate for American men is four times higher in retirement than in any other stage of life.[5] *USA Today* recently reported in an article, "Planning for a Longer Retirement", that although many enjoy the first few years of retirement, optimism soon drops. The proportion of satisfied retirees sinks from nearly eighty percent in the first phase of retirement to below sixty-five percent. Limited finances and illness may affect these statistics, but they also show that there is more to life than fishing and golf. A friend of mine put it this way, "Leisure is only as good as the friction against it." Leisure time is like money and popularity; once you have it in abundance, it loses much of its attraction. Most people need some kind of rewarding, consistent work as long as they are physically able.

Consistency in Self-Care

Every morning, Clarence Custer, age ninety, hits the tennis courts. Some days he plays for an hour and a half. On better days he plays for three hours. Plus, three times a week he hikes over to the local gym and lifts weights. He is so active, he was asked to carry the torch for the 2002 Winter Olympics. (*AARP Magazine*)

What a contrast to the guy who wrote the exercise diary found at the beginning of this chapter. Which one comes closer to describing your lifestyle?

Exercise not only keeps our heart and lungs strong and our joints and muscles flexible, it reduces stress. The endorphins released by exercise give us a feeling of well-being and contentment. But exercise, like other healthy habits, must be done consistently with a commitment to excellence.

We will discuss some of the particulars of physical health in more detail in the next chapter on strategy. But during this season when our health will likely decline to some degree, be diligent about habits such as exercise, eating healthy foods, taking supplements, and getting regular health exams.

The Rewards of Consistency

Shirley

Consistency is a vital key for significance, but it reaps countless other rewards, too. I'd like to share a story about some close friends of ours, Mike and Linda. When their third child Ronnie was born, the baby lost his hearing because of an erroneous medical procedure. As parents of this profoundly deaf child, Linda and Mike had to make some decisions about Ronnie's education and training.

There was much pressure to teach Ronnie sign language, but his mom and dad wanted him to be part of the hearing world. He constantly tried to speak.

They knew if he learned sign language, he would probably never speak. So they found a "retired" teacher who taught Ronnie the oral method of communication. Ronnie never learned signing and was never a part of the deaf community. Mike and Linda were sorely misunderstood and received a lot of criticism for their decision.

But Ronnie became a great lip reader and learned to speak surprisingly well. He was mainstreamed at the public school in their small Texas community. In third grade, Ronnie started falling behind. So one day Linda just showed up at school. She would mouth the words of the teacher when her back was turned so Ronnie could continue to "hear" her. Ronnie's grades started improving immediately. Linda continued going to school with Ronnie every single day — third through twelfth grade. Ronnie not only graduated in the upper third of his class, he excelled at football and went on to junior college.

Linda's is the best example of consistency and commitment I can think of. She put aside any career plans of her own and went to school with her son. When Ronnie graduated from high school, Linda received an honorary diploma, too. She doesn't regret a single day.

Today, Ronnie is happily married to a hearing person and runs a successful business. Several years ago, with the introduction of the cochlear implant technology, Ronnie learned he was a perfect candidate for the surgery. He is now beginning to hear sounds for the first time in his life and is expected to develop about eighty percent hearing over time. It is truly a medical miracle, but if Ronnie had not been taught to speak when he was young, he would not have been a good candidate for the technology. He would never have been able to hear his new daughter call him "daddy." Linda was misunderstood, but her consistency paid off.

There are huge rewards for a life of consistency: personal discipline, a feeling of self worth, spiritual maturity, better physical health, and close personal relationships. Be consistent; don't settle for less than excellence.

Action Steps to Develop Godly Habits:

• *Develop a plan to evaluate your consistency in all areas of life. Suggestion: Be accountable to a pastor or close friend and take stock regularly.*

• *Make daily prayer and Bible study a habitual, consistent part of your schedule.*

• *Practice listening during your prayer sessions, and write down what you believe God is saying to you along with any personal directives you get from scripture.*

• *Evaluate your relationship with your spouse, children, and friends. Have you become negligent in your effort to grow these relationships? Devise a plan for more consistency and more connection.*

• *If you no longer work full time, evaluate your personal work habits and self-care. Make an effort to be just as consistent in meaningful use of your time.*

• *Give regularly of your money and time to God's work and to the needy.*

Suggested Reading

Total Forgiveness, R. T. Kendall

The Eve Factor, Shirley Rose

From Success to Significance, Lloyd Reeb

Once a Parent Always a Parent, Stephen A. Bly

Mid Course Correction, Gordon MacDonald

Staying Young and Fit

The best way to stay young is to eat right, exercise, and lie about your age.

*The thirty day diet is quite popular — that's the one people
are going to start in about thirty days.*

If you're pushing sixty, that's exercise enough.

Forget about eating natural foods; I need all the preservatives I can get.

*If God had wanted me to touch my toes,
He would have put them on my knees.*

*The older you get, the tougher it is to lose weight,
because your body and your fat are really good friends.*

*I gave up jogging for my health when my thighs kept
rubbing together and set my pantyhose on fire.*

*One of life's mysteries is how a two-pound box of candy
can make a woman gain five pounds.*

*Amazing! You hang something in your closet for awhile
and it shrinks two sizes.*

*Skinny people irritate me, especially when they say things like,
"I forgot to eat." I've forgotten my address, my maiden name,
and my keys, but never forgot to eat.*

Blessed are they who hunger and thirst, for they are sticking to their diet.

*Inside this fat person is a thin person struggling to get out;
but she can usually be sedated with a few pieces of chocolate.*

Fourth Coordinate:
Strategy
A Plan to Turn Aging into Significance

Where there is no vision the people perish…

Proverbs 29:18

Jerry

The Melrose suspension bridge above the Niagara Falls links the United States and Canada. The bridge was engineered and built by Theodore Elliot in 1948. Some thought it would be impossible to span the distance. But Elliot had a strategy.

First, he flew a kite across the span with a thread attached. Next, a thin cord was tied to the thread, and it was pulled across. Then a rope was attached to the cord, and the rope was pulled across. Finally, a strong cable was pulled across, and the process of building the bridge began. What started with a tiny thread ended with an engineering marvel.

Aging + Strategy = Potential for Significance

In order to find significance, we need a plan, a strategy for the second half of life. It doesn't have to be a grandiose plan — the details can be filled in later — but we have to begin with a strategy. Ideally this plan should be formulated years before retirement age. However, it is never too late to devise a strategy for the rest of your life.

If you decide to build a house, you can go to a well-stocked home improvement center and find just about everything you need. You can buy lumber, drywall, tools, concrete, plumbing and electrical supplies, tile, screws, and nails. But you will never get a house from those materials unless you have a blueprint, a strategy for building it. With a strategy, you have everything you need for a *potential* structure. It will become a house, of course, when someone with the skill and expertise ultimately carries out the plan.

Jesus had a strategy for evangelizing the world. First, He kept a low profile until John the Baptist had completed his ministry of announcing Jesus's arrival. Second, He went to John to be baptized. Next, Jesus went into the wilderness to pray and fast for forty days. (What an important lesson for us as we begin a ministry or plan for the future) There He soundly defeated Satan, setting the stage for His successful mission. Next, Jesus chose His disciples. When He had gathered the twelve, He began to train and prepare them for three years. They learned continuously by observing His ministry and by the wise teaching and instruction He gave them. They learned valuable lessons of both boldness and humility. They learned consistency in prayer. Their faith was increased as they watched the supernatural miracles.

After the crucifixion and the resurrection, as Jesus was preparing to leave the disciples, He implemented the final steps of His strategy. He commissioned the disciples to carry on His ministry, to reach the world for Christ, and to train future generations. (Mark 16:15-20, Matthew 28:19) When He had returned to heaven, He sent the Holy Spirit to be their helper and guide. Jesus not only had a plan, He carried it out — and it was incredibly successful.

Vision

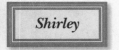

How do you begin to formulate your strategy for the next half of your life? Well, begin by thinking of something you have always wanted to do, but haven't been able to accomplish. Is there an idea you've kept on the back burner for years? Before you can come up with a good plan, you have to have a destination in mind. That goal is called a *vision* or a dream for the future. Ideally, your vision will be birthed in much prayer for God's will.

Is your primary goal not to set goals? Are you afraid to set goals because you always seem to fail, and you don't want to be disappointed? Do you want to set realistic goals but don't know how? You are not alone.

It's surprising how many people cannot verbalize a vision — possibly because it does not exist. Lack of vision is one of the greatest mistakes of the fifty plus crowd. I found myself in that situation at midlife because most of my dreams had been tied up in my children. More than anything, I wanted

Jeff, Trevor, and Vanessa to be educated, happily married, and self-supporting. Generation X taught us that young adults get to those milestones later and later these days. But once my three children were married and out of the house, I realized I needed a plan for *my* future.

I shared in Chapter One how my television program was born and how an old dream of becoming a writer came true. But I was fortunate. God allowed me to be at the right place at the right time for these opportunities to present themselves, and I have worked very hard to make the most of them. But I didn't have a good plan. I could have wandered, without direction, like so many empty nesters. I'm glad I now have a pretty clear vision for the future, but I expect those goals to change and grow with the years.

If you don't feel any particular leading toward a goal or vision, perhaps you need to do a little homework. Everyone needs to start somewhere. Here are some questions to ask yourself as you begin to think about the second half of life:

1. *What activities make you feel happy, energized, and valuable?*
2. *If you could spend your life doing anything you wanted, what would it be?*
3. *Is there some secret desire that is buried deep inside that perhaps you haven't even shared with anyone?*
4. *Do you have a calling from God that you've never been able to fulfill?*
5. *What gifts, talents, or resources do you have that are not being used?*
6. *Is there something you could do now to start preparing yourself (such as get more education, learn a skill, or revamp your resume)?*
7. *How would this goal affect your family and financial situation?*
8. *How important is it to you to spend time serving others?*

This is by no means an exhaustive list. But many people don't have clear cut goals because they believe the enemy's lie that their dream is too big, too difficult, or that there are too many obstacles to prevent it from becoming reality.

How do you eat an elephant? One bite at a time. It's important to solidify your dreams by writing them down and discussing them with someone. It becomes easier to overcome obstacles if they can be reduced to bite-sized pieces. A negative perspective can become a hopeful one. Often, people keep their dreams buried because they feel inadequate or fearful. Never underestimate what God can do with your life when you are fully committed to Him.

"For I know the plans I have for you," declares the Lord, "plans to prosper you and not to harm you, plans to give you hope and a future." (Jeremiah 29:11) (NIV)

Dream God's Dream

Once you get a clear vision, how do you know if the dream is worthy, on track, and in line with God's will? It's important to make sure we are not driven to accomplish our vision for selfish purposes. Some have well-thought-out goals and a thorough strategy for accomplishing them. But their motivation is money, power, or fame. That kind of success is of the world and one of the reasons many wealthy, successful people turn to philanthropic ventures in the search for peace and meaning. When they have acquired everything they want, they are still empty and unfulfilled.

That's why it is so important to *dream God's dream* for you. Proverbs 16: 9 (NIV) warns, "In his heart a man plans his course, but the Lord determines his steps." Allow God to be a part of your plan and strategy. If you doubt that the voice you are hearing is really God's, perhaps this little self-quiz will help. Ask yourself each question, and answer honestly:

1. *Does your vision for the future conform to God's Word? If you want to do something unethical, immoral, or contrary to the Bible, the vision is not from God.*
2. *Are your dreams focused around your own personal preferences, selfish motives, or ambitions? In God's perfect ecology, He will usually direct us toward what we are good at and what we enjoy doing. But we must analyze our motives and get out of our comfort zone when necessary.*

95

3. *How emotional are you about this subject? Are your emotions dominating your choices? Prayerfully keep an open mind and heart.*

4. *Will following this leading enhance your spiritual life or detract from it? More than any Kingdom work you might accomplish, God is more interested in your personal relationship with Him. Who you are is more important than what you do.*

5. *What do your godly counselors say? The advice of others cannot drive our decisions, but we should listen prayerfully to others' perspectives. "Where no counsel is, the people fall: but in the multitude of counselors there is safety." (Proverbs 11:14) (KJV)*

6. *Does this leading grow out of a pattern of prayer, Bible study, and your relationship with the Lord? Or have you made assumptions based on what you want?*

7. *Who will benefit most from this action: God's Kingdom, or you, or both?*

8. *Are you willing to do whatever God asks of you?*

Keep in mind there is nothing wrong with saying to God, "I'm confused. I don't have a clear picture. Please show me!" And God has every right to say, "It's not time yet. Just wait and prepare yourself." God said to His prophet: *But these things I plan won't happen right away. Slowly, steadily, surely, the time approaches when the vision will be fulfilled. If it seems slow, do not despair, for these things will surely come to pass. Just be patient! They will not be overdue a single day!* (Habakkuk 2:3) (TLB)

There are times when we must re-evaluate our plans and admit that perhaps we've missed God's will. It has certainly happened to me. And we all have to re-evaluate or adjust our vision over time. When you are fifty, your vision for the future will obviously be different than it is at sixty-five or seventy-five. But you will always accomplish more if you have a plan.

If your goals line up with God's plan for you, then you can move forward with your strategy, assured of success because you will have divine guidance — a GPS far better than any satellite — to help you find your way. Another reason to seek God's plan is because God usually has a far bigger dream for you than you could imagine.

Planning Your Strategy

There are several steps to planning a successful strategy. First, figure out what God wants you to do. Second, lay out the logical plan of action it will take to get there. We often begin with incomplete information, and some of what we plan might be based on mere speculation. But it still helps to have a strategy broken down into components of the first step, second step, and so on, making adjustments as necessary.

For example, you might decide that God wants you to work with prisoners. It has been your secret calling, but you have no idea how to begin. Here is what your strategy might look like.

1. *Do research on your own about the prison system and prison ministry. Then contact your pastor or someone you know who does prison ministry. Find out if there are opportunities to volunteer, and get the details. You could call the correctional institution, but it is much better to connect with someone who has done what you want to do — an important strategy for any new venture.*

2. *Take an honest look at your credentials. Do you have experience speaking to groups? (The prisoners could be a difficult audience.) Have you taught Bible studies or done inspirational sermons? Are you spiritually mature? If you need more education or experience, or to find a spiritual mentor, plan a strategy for getting what you need.*

3. *See if you can go along with a group who does prison ministry. Serve in any way you can, and learn as you observe. Gradually you can take on more of a leadership role.*

4. *Finally, if you have the necessary requirements, you can move to becoming a chaplain for the prison system in your area.*

These are only four steps, but it is a strategy that could take months or years to implement. But the joy of fulfilling God's calling for the second half of life is worth any sacrifice, hard work, or obstacle you must overcome.

You might decide that you've always wanted to take short-term missions trips to other countries. Your strategy might need to include ways to earn enough money to pay your way. As part of your strategy, write down ways you could earn the extra money to begin to travel. Ask God to provide, but be willing to do your part.

Your strategy might include taking a Bible class, enrolling in college courses, or locating to another area. If you are having a difficult time coming up with a vision for the future or long term goals, ask God to direct you. At least you can have a general plan such as: I want to keep working in some capacity, I want to stay active, I want to be involved in Kingdom work, I want to have more interaction with my grandkids, etc.

These are very general ideas, but sometimes the details fill in a little at a time. Your strategy might be to start spending extra time in prayer and possibly fasting until you get direction. Keep your heart open, and have your antennae up to recognize an opportunity when it comes your way.

The Granny Brigade

Miriam Machovec had never been one to sit around doing nothing. And now as a great-grandmother in her seventies, that hasn't changed. She marched onto our *Aspiring Women* set in a gorgeous coral suit and stunning jewelry that my co-hosts and I could envy. She is an adorable, petite blonde with deep dimples, beautiful brown eyes, and a heart-stopping smile. She looks ten years younger than her age and exudes energy and enthusiasm.

Miriam and her husband were the successful owners of apartment buildings and nursing homes. At the age of forty-seven, her husband fell asleep at the wheel of his car and was killed. Miriam says that as a widow with three children, the youngest of which was twelve years old, she just did what she had to do a day at a time.

After working and raising her children alone, Miriam faced retirement. But she just couldn't imagine slowing down. She had been raised on a farm and always worked hard. Even though she didn't have a concrete plan at that point, her goal was to stay busy, hopefully doing some meaningful work. Keeping her ears and eyes open for opportunities, she took advantage of a chance to go on a mission trip. She enjoyed it so much she got hooked — and she identified a great need. With her vision suddenly coming into view, Miriam planned her strategy.

She gathered a group of seven other grandmothers to travel to Africa with her. While talking with a friend about it, she said she was forming "The Granny Brigade." She was shocked to hear the words come out of her mouth because she didn't even know the definition of "brigade." She looked it up and discovered it means a group of people with a purpose to accomplish much. She thought that was fitting, so the name stuck.

The Granny Brigade traveled to South Africa where their primary purpose was to touch, hold, rock, and just love on orphaned children. These were AIDS orphans, and some of the children were HIV positive. The epidemic has so devastated some portions of Africa that entire tribes could be extinct within ten to fifteen years. The grannies visited one little community of shanties where all the inhabitants were children. One child of twelve was taking care of nine siblings. Miriam talks with fond memories of the beautiful babies who are so needy. She says they are starved for love and just cling to you. She says, "We are the only grandmothers they will ever have."

Miriam is now a full-time volunteer for "Book of Hope," which supplies a comic book version of the gospel in many languages, and she is anxiously awaiting her next trip to Africa. She is living significantly.

Three Pillars of Health

In order to plan an effective strategy, there are some basic principles in your life that must be in place. Without a solid foundation, any vision, strategy, or implementation will fail. We mentioned the analogy of building a house. Even if you have a great blueprint for the building, if the foundation is not secure, the house will eventually crumble and fall. Scripture tells us, "Through wisdom a house is built, and by understanding it is established; by knowledge the rooms are filled with all precious and pleasant riches." (Proverbs 24:3, 4) The remainder of this chapter will address the elements that make up the foundation on which your significance can be built.

As we discussed in the first chapter, there are three primary pillars of health that need to be considered when planning a strategy for significance. The triad includes spiritual health, physical health, and financial health. As we consider these three areas, let's revisit the concept of the GPS, Global Positioning System.

If you remember, there are three satellites that beam the signals to fix our position. The first of the three pinpoints our position within about six hundred miles. That's a pretty small circle when you consider the size of the earth. The second narrows our location even more. But it is the exact intersection of the three circles that identifies our precise location.

It is a fitting analogy to consider our spiritual GPS, God's Plan for Significance, as also having three essential components, spiritual health, physical health, and financial health. All three are important and perform their own function, but when we have all three of these "satellites" in perfect alignment, we can pinpoint where we are in our quest for significance. Let's look at a strategy for these three areas.

Spiritual Health

What does a strategy for spiritual health look like? You've read much in this book on spiritual growth because it's one of the most critically important keys to significance. You may not be able to look back at a specific time and day when you began your spiritual journey. Perhaps you just grew up in church, and the things of God became more important through the years. But we all have to begin somewhere.

I recently interviewed Lynn Hybels for *Aspiring Women.* She is the wife of Bill Hybels, the pastor of Willow Creek Church, one of the largest churches in the world. Lynn shares in her book, *Nice Girls Don't Change the World,* that even as a young girl she always loved God and wanted to serve Him. When she married Bill, she immersed herself in ministry, always working and striving to please God. But when she turned fifty years old, she realized she didn't even like the God she had always known. She saw God as a strict, demanding tyrant who always wanted more than she could give.

Lynn went through months of depression and burn out, resisting even the idea of God. Finally, when her body and emotions began to heal, she experienced a longing for God again. Not the God of her childhood, but *some* God. Alone at night, she began to feel a *loving* presence around her. As she opened her heart a tiny crack, she sensed God saying:

I love you. I love you so much I want you to rest ... I want you to know that all those years when you were working so hard to try to please me, I was trying to tell you to slow down ... I wasn't the one cracking the whip ... the one who made you feel guilty when you relaxed ... I was the one trying to love you.[1]

You may be unhealthy spiritually because you have an incorrect view of God. You may have grown up in a spiritual environment that was heavy on judgment and light on grace. God loves you and wants more than anything for you to have freedom, joy, and purpose in your life. Spiritual health begins when you get to know God's character.

On the other hand, God is a holy God. He has provided for our salvation through Christ's death and resurrection. But we are responsible for spiritual growth.

Jerry

Once we have a healthy view of God and are trying to reflect Christ in our life, what does the rest of the strategy look like? There are several basic elements. It's first about transformation and relationship, and then the good works follow.

1. *Salvation:* If you are not absolutely sure where you stand with God, symbolically nail down a stake in the ground by making things right. Romans 10:9 gives us two simple but profound steps toward transformation. First, confess your sins, and secondly, believe that the risen Christ can forgive them. Then you will never have to wonder again, because if you believe, then you will receive. (John 3:16-18)

2. *Church attendance:* As we discussed in the last chapter on consistency, it is critically important to attend a church that teaches the Bible. Not only do you need to be fed a regular dose of teaching on God's Word, but you need the fellowship of other believers.

3. *Involvement with church activities and volunteering your service:* Too many Christians only attend church once a week and feel their obligation to church is met. But each member of the body has a job to do. Make yourself available. Your strategy might include meeting with the pastor or pastor's wife to see where you might be needed.

4. *Prayer and personal time with God:* We've talked much about prayer already. But it is an essential element in spiritual health. Communication in any relationship is critical, and if you find yourself spiritually weak, you probably need more deep interaction with the Lord. Take whatever steps necessary to make it happen.

5. *Bible study:* You don't have to be a scholar to develop a deep love and appreciation for God's Word. But again, this takes planning, discipline, and determination. Read your Bible daily, and keep a notebook or electronic file of the insights you receive. Try to attend a Bible study class once or twice a month, and memorize one verse per week. I remember so well the final days of my mother's life. She was very weak and near death. One day, she suddenly began to quote scripture. She went on and on for several minutes, reciting every verse she could remember. I don't know what kind of spiritual battle she was fighting, but I know her knowledge of the Bible helped her in her last hours.

6. *Share your faith:* This is an area that is difficult for most of us. And I believe it gets even harder as we get older. I remember conducting street meetings when I was a young man. Shirley tells of how she used to go door to door to share her faith with strangers. But she admits she would be more reluctant to do that kind of evangelism today. The good news is you don't have to share your faith that way — unless God specifically directs you to. But we do need to prayerfully seek opportunities to tell others about Christ.

7. *Give generously:* We've already discussed the value of giving of your time through volunteering at your church or in your community. But we must also have a strategy for giving of our finances to God's work and other good causes. Give to your church, and help the needy. Sponsor a child overseas, give to missions, give to needy friends, or all of the above. Plan a strategy; then be faithful to give.

The disciplines of prayer, Bible study, church attendance, witnessing, and giving must be done regularly, consistently with a commitment to excellence. As they become a part of your life, you will be spiritually healthy.

Physical Health

Shirley

It is interesting that godly habits can actually bring about better physical health. *Spokesman Review* reported that people who practice their religious faith regularly may be getting some earthly benefits: They appear to be healthier compared to people who never attend a house of worship. Spiritual health and physical health are definitely interrelated. And physical health is a must for successful aging. What does a strategy for physical health look like?

Mark Twain said, "The only way to keep your health is to eat what you don't want, drink what you don't like, and do what you'd rather not." I'm afraid it's sad, but true. Most of us would prefer to eat junk food, drink good-tasting, sweet drinks, and be inactive — rather than eat healthy, drink enough water, and exercise. You may believe that every person has a number of days allotted by God, and when that number's up, he or she will leave this earth. "So," you may ask, "why demand so much of myself? I will die anyway when it's my time to go." You might wonder what exercise and healthy diets have to do with significance.

First, we have an obligation to view our body as the temple of the Holy Spirit. We should consider it a gift that is entrusted to our care. (1 Corinthians 6: 19) Second, personal discipline builds character. As we emphasized in the last chapter on consistency, a significant life is one that is characterized by healthy habits. And finally, if we are to spend the final decades of our lives in meaningful Kingdom work, we must stay as healthy as possible. Yes, illness will come. Aches and pains go with the territory. But we should not assume, or let our doctor assume, that physical limitations are inevitable.

A dear friend of ours, who we affectionately called Grandma Margaret, was well into her seventies when she began to have some hip pain. After her doctor had examined her, she expected a diagnosis. Her doctor said, "Well, Margaret, after all, that hip joint *is* over seventy years old."

"Yes," Margaret replied, "but so is my other hip. And it's not hurting!" Don't just accept physical limitations, and don't take them lying down. And never forget that God is the great physician. (Psalm 103:3)

A healthy physical body is like a healthy spiritual life in that it really just takes a few basics. But the healthy habits must be done consistently with a commitment to excellence. Here are a few of the health basics:

1. ***Eat a healthy diet and maintain proper weight.*** When I say "diet," I don't mean a short-term plan to lose weight; I'm referring to your overall eating plan. There are many good books available to help you plan a diet that is appropriate for your age, metabolic type, and physical needs. See the reading list at the end of the chapter for some helpful guide books. And talk to your doctor or nutritionist.

2. ***Take supplements:*** We all know that our foods alone do not give us the nutrition we need. Even medical doctors, historically skeptical about the benefits of vitamins, are now prescribing supplements for good health. The data is undeniable. You need vitamins, minerals, antioxidants, and more. I have found the whole supplement question to be overwhelming. That's why TLN, after years of research, found a Christian company that offers very high potency, high quality products. The best news is that *Kylea Health and Energy* has developed a complete, one formula, powdered drink mix that provides everything we need in one daily serving. It contains both supplements and four to five servings of dark, leafy greens. Jerry and I have been taking this product for years, and the results have been dramatic — increased energy, better elimination, weight control,

and the peace of mind that we are getting maximum nutrition. We highly recommend it.[2] If you are to be consistent about taking supplements, the plan must be simple and doable, but taking supplements is absolutely vital for good health.

3. *Exercise:* According to *American Health,* regular exercise toughens the mind as well as the body. After working out three times a week for six months, one group was found to be twenty percent fitter, but the surprising bonus — they also scored seventy percent better on a test of complex decision making. (as quoted in *Homemade*, November 1985) Well, it's one thing to know about exercise; it's another thing altogether to be consistent about *doing* it. Exercise is hard. It's exhausting. But it is necessary. According to the National Institute on Aging, inactive people lose capability because they've stagnated, not because they're getting older. Older, inactive adults lose ground in four areas that are important to staying healthy and independent — endurance, strength, balance, and flexibility. Each can be maintained through regular exercise such as dancing. If you can't stand traditional exercise classes or the treadmill, your strategy could include more enjoyable activities such as dance, swimming, or water aerobics. But, at the very least, you can establish a regimen of brisk walking several times a week. If you are going to stay healthy, you have no option but to exercise. Talk to your doctor first, and get a medical exam. Then, when you begin your exercise program, schedule it on your calendar and be consistent. Another great help in motivation is a partner. Someone to talk to makes exercise more enjoyable and gives you accountability for staying consistent.

4. *Get enough rest:* I find as I get older, sleep doesn't come as easily for me as it once did. I also reason that since I'm well into the second half of life, why do I want to waste time sleeping? But we all need to give our bodies a chance to repair and rebuild through sleep. Regular rest periods

throughout the day are also needed if we are doing strenuous work.

5. ***Drink plenty of water:*** Most sources agree that we should drink one-half our body weight in ounces per day. If you weigh 130 pounds, for instance, you need sixty-five ounces of water per day. That is about eight glasses. The hydration keeps our cells healthy, gives us energy, and helps eliminate toxins from our system.

6. ***Keep a balance between work and play:*** Yes, part of your strategy for significance is consistent work, but a balanced strategy must include consistent play. Don't let your passion for work crowd out recreation, hobbies, fellowship, laughter, and just having fun. It is a vital part of physical health.

Since medical science has wiped out many of the fatal diseases of the past, in the twenty-first century it is often our own personal choices that determine our health. Choices about alcohol, drugs, inactivity, smoking, sexual conduct, and other similar issues now have a greater affect on life than any other single factor. With this in mind, here are a few other factors to keep in mind as you develop a strategy for physical health.

Key Factors in Physical Health

1. *Assume a sense of responsibility for your own health, and be pro-active, not passive. This means regular checkups with doctor and dentist, as well as procedures such as mammograms, pap smears, colonoscopies, PSA count for prostate, and screenings for diabetes, bone loss, glaucoma, hearing loss, etc. Listen to your body. Don't be too proud to get things checked out when you sense something is wrong.*

2. *Learn to manage stress. Though the second half of life should ideally offer lighter work load and less stress, that is not always the reality. The elimination of as much stress as possible can lengthen your life.*

3. *Maintain a healthy self-image, and interact with other people in a rewarding and healthy manner.*

4. *Understand sexuality, and develop satisfying intimate relationships.*

5. *Avoid tobacco, drugs, and excessive alcohol.*

6. *Know the facts about cardiovascular disease, cancer, infections,*
   sexually transmitted diseases, and the potential for injury.
   Use that knowledge to protect yourself from them.

7. *Learn as much as you can about the health care system,*
   and use it intelligently.

8. *Know when to treat your illness yourself and when to seek help.*[3]

Your Overall Wellness Profile

In addition to these key factors, the following elements are an indication of overall good health. See how many of these are present in your life and how many you can incorporate.

1. *Presence of a strong support network.*

2. *Consistent sense of positive expectations.*

3. *Episodic outbursts of joyful, happy experiences.*

4. *Strong spiritual involvement.*

5. *Adaptability to changing circumstances.*

6. *Tendency to identify and communicate feelings.*

7. *Regular expression of gratitude and generosity.*

8. *Persistent sense of humor.*[4]

One overriding fact must be kept in mind: our bodies do grow old and wear out over time. Two thoughts can help you prepare in advance for the inevitable. The first is "ready or not!" The second is "like it or not!" Everyone must deal with the fact that at any moment the phone call may come from the doctor with bad news or a serious diagnosis. Chest pains, dizziness, or worse symptoms may force you into an immediate whirlwind of activity for you, your spouse, or your parents. If you are mentally prepared for this, it will keep you from feeling overwhelmed, and you will never be taken completely by surprise.

The Bible refers to our bodies as "jars of clay," fragile, easily broken, and temporary. But here's the good news:

"But we have this treasure in jars of clay to show that this all-surpassing power is from God and not from us. We are hard pressed on every side, but not crushed; perplexed, but not in despair; persecuted, but not abandoned; struck down, but not destroyed. We always carry around in our body the death of Jesus, so that the life of Jesus may also be revealed in our body." (2 Corinthians 4:7)

God has chosen our fragile bodies to house the glory of Jesus himself. It is reason enough to do our best to take good care of them. The bottom line is to have a strategy. Live a balanced life. And leave the rest in God's hands.

Financial Health

Much has been written about finances and financial health. Christian and secular bookstores have shelves of books and materials about this critical subject. There are some financial counselors who claim that the Bible has more to say about money than any other single topic. Obviously, the issue of finances is an important issue and has a major impact on what you are able to do and enjoy in your second half. Randy Swanson, attorney and CFO for Total Living International, shares the following insights on financial health at his seminars and with individual clients.

The first consideration in planning your strategy is to understand three critical Biblical principles regarding finances. The first principle is a proper attitude toward money. The second is to obey the clear commands of scripture regarding finances. And the third is to keep a proper balance regarding our finances. These three can be remembered by the letters **BOA** — balance, obedience, and attitude. Just like a Boa Constrictor, your aging years can have the significance and joy squeezed right out if these three principles are not followed diligently. They must form the foundation of your financial strategy

Balance: Scripture tells us to keep balance in our finances. Not to have too much so that we forget about God and not to have so little that we have to steal. He will supply all of our needs. We came into the world with nothing, and we will leave it with nothing. Greed is a sin, and significant, joyful living is not related to how much money we have. (Proverbs 30:6, 9; Philippians 4:6-12; 1 Timothy 6:7, 8; Luke 12:15)

Obedience: We must be obedient to the clear teaching of scripture. The Bible teaches us that we cannot serve two masters, God and money. If we are trustworthy with little, God will give us more. If we are faithful with other people's money, we will be trusted with more of our own. The Word says that the man who builds his house on the rock, a solid foundation, is the one who hears God's instructions and then *does what He says*. It is God who teaches us how to prosper and directs us in the use of our money. (Luke 16:10-13; Luke 6:46-49; Isaiah 48:17; Matthew 28:20; 1 John 5:3)

Attitude: Scripture tells us to guard our attitude about money. We are stewards and not owners. The love of money is the root of all sorts of evil. We are not to become rich by extortion or robbery. We are warned that when we have plenty, we are in danger of forgetting the Lord and all of His provision. The bottom line is we must maintain an attitude of dependence on God and *not* become ambitious for wealth to the neglect of our spiritual health. (1 Timothy 6:9, 17; Proverbs 16:1-3; Proverbs 11: 28; Psalm 62:10; Deuteronomy 8:11-19) Answer the following questions to get a handle on your true attitude about money:

1. *How do I view money, and how does it make me feel? Is it a means to an end or is it my goal?*
2. *Am I living beyond my means?*
3. *Have I allowed my career to crowd out other important priorities?*
4. *Do I feel I have to make a certain amount in order to be considered smart and successful?*

5. Have I had peace or been depressed during times of financial need?

6. How much of my money do I give to God's work and others in need?

There are many practical strategies for dealing with our finances, but unless the three basic principles of balance, obedience, and attitude are in proper order, no strategy will be successful.

Here are some specific steps to help you gain control of your finances and enhance your possibilities in the second half of life:

1. *Save aggressively.* If you have begun saving late in life, you should try to save up to twenty-five percent of your take home pay. Another way to save is to have two incomes and save one.

2. *Live on a budget.* Even the most simplistic budget written on a scrap of paper will do wonders to control your spending.

3. *Maximize 401K plans, matching programs from your employer, or your own individual IRA account.* Special rules are in place for late starters to catch up with extra contribution limits for IRA accounts.

4. *Work longer to provide income and be able to save.* Today, the span between fifty-five and seventy is enough time to create a nest egg, especially with the marvel of compound interest. Also, the labor laws now protect you and encourage employers to hire older adults so a change to an easier job or a part-time job is possible.

5. *Learn to multi-task.* Involve yourself in things that have multiple returns, such as a college degree that can pave the way to do some teaching at a later time in life. Or a hobby that can make you money, such as photography or crafts that can be sold. Maybe your situation will lend itself to creating a home-based business now or in the future.

6. *Take advantage of home equity.* Consider moving to a less expensive location so that your equity will pay off a home in your new location. Moving from either coast of the United States toward the central states will almost always create a savings in living expense.

7. Use credit sparingly and wisely. One definition of credit is the difference between your income and your desired lifestyle. As you approach a time of fixed income, you must be extremely cautious in the use of credit cards. All too frequently, aging adults face the embarrassment of bankruptcy because of out-of-control credit debt.

8. Consider a job that gives back. Jobs such as writing, journalism, teaching, tutoring, substituting, and house sitting are not demanding physically and can usually be done part time.

9. Find and join an investment club. There are many on the Internet or listed in the newspaper. Others with expertise and success can help you start a simple investment program where you can increase your net income over what you get from merely a bank account.

10. Get a clear picture of social security and other government benefits. There are many benefits that you have paid for all of your working life for which you are eligible. Many never collect on this income because they don't know about it.

Finally, there are a number of issues that should be looked at as they relate to you personally. Part of your strategy should be to become knowledgeable and informed about these areas of financial life and how they might impact your future.

1. Credit Protection

2. Social Security

3. Long Term Care Insurance

4. Financial Elder Abuse

5. Estate Planning

6. Late Retirement Planning

7. Leaving a Meaningful Financial Legacy

If you have acquired health in these three critical areas: spiritual, physical, and financial, then you have a solid foundation for significance. Identify your dream, purify your vision by earnestly seeking God's will, then plan a step-by-step strategy. Next — get ready for the action!

Action Steps for a Successful Strategy:

• *Begin to build your spiritual foundation by accepting Christ.*

• *Find a good church, and be faithful in attendance. Find areas of service that you can fill. Plan a time for regular Bible study and prayer. Build a strategy for planned, regular giving of finances. And look for opportunities to witness.*

• *Maintain physical health through diet, exercise, health care, and proper mental attitude.*

• *Do your best to strengthen your finances through Biblical principles and wise investments.*

• *Identify your goals and vision, and purify your dreams through seeking God's will.*

• *Plan a practical step-by-step strategy for reaching your goals.*

Suggested Reading

The Great Physician's Rx for Health and Wellness, Jordan S. Rubin

Holy Hormones!, J. Ron Eaker M.D.

Wealth to Last, Larry Burkett & Ron Blue

Money and Possessions: the Quest for Contentment, Kay Arthur and David Arthur

Second Calling, Dale Henson Bourke

Living the Extraordinary Life, Charles F. Stanley

The 7 Sins of Highly Defective People, Rick Ezell

Knowing God, J. I. Packer

A Poem of Gratitude

I have never made a fortune,
And I'm sure it's too late now,
But I don't worry much about that;
I'm happy anyhow.
As I journey on life's way,
I'm reaping better than I sowed.
I'm drinking from my saucer,
'Cause my cup has overflowed.

Haven't got a lot of riches,
And sometimes the going's tough.
But I've got loving ones around me,
And that makes me rich enough.
I thank God for all his blessings,
And the mercies He's bestowed.
I'm drinking from my saucer,
'Cause my cup has overflowed.

I remember times when things went wrong,
My faith was somewhat thin.
But all at once the dark clouds broke,
And the sun peeped through again.
So, Lord, help me not to gripe
About the tough rows I have hoed.
I'm drinking from my saucer,
'Cause my cup has overflowed.

If God gives me strength and courage,
When the way grows steep and rough,
I'll not ask for other blessings,
I'm already blessed enough.
And may I never be too busy
To help others bear their loads.
I'll keep drinking from my saucer,
'Cause my cup has overflowed.

7

Fifth Coordinate:
Action
Just Do It!

So, dear brothers, work hard to prove that you really are among those God has called and chosen, and then you will never stumble and fall away.

2 Peter 1:10 (TLB)

Late one evening, a professor sorted his mail when a magazine caught his attention with the title, "The Needs of the Congo Mission." The educator was consumed by these words: "The need is great here. We have no one to work in the northern province of Gabon in the central Congo." The professor closed the magazine and wrote, "My search is over." The famous scholar and concert musician began training as a medical missionary. His name was Albert Schweitzer.[1]

At that point, Schweitzer had already had two successful careers — musician and theologian. He then became a jungle doctor and by age thirty-six had established his hospital in Gabon, French West Africa. There, he practiced humbly until he was captured and held as an enemy alien by the French during World War I. When he was released, he was approaching fifty, and his hospital lay in ruins. No one could have faulted him for returning to an easier life. But he decided to rebuild the hospital, which he ran until his death at age ninety.[2]

Albert Schweitzer has always been one of my heroes. He responded to God's call through inspirational faith and was not afraid to make major changes in the direction of his life. He was willing to create a strategy, prepare himself through more education, and see his vision fulfilled. Even after dire hardship and years of imprisonment, he took action to re-build his hospital in order to sacrificially help others. In the last decades of his life, he continued to live significantly.

If You Want a Horse Buy a Saddle

When my daughter was about nine years old, she began horseback riding lessons. I had loved horses since my childhood but never owned one. I started thinking about a strategy to get a horse for her. When I mentioned it to my wife, she sensibly pointed out that finances were very tight. And even if we could find a reasonably priced horse, we must think of stable fees, tack, farrier, and veterinarian charges, not to mention all the unknown expenses a horse might incur. She was right, of course.

One day, Vanessa and I went to a farm auction just for fun, and I came home with a saddle. My wife looked at it and said, "Jerry, that's a nice saddle, but you don't have a horse."

But part of my strategy was *if you want a horse, buy a saddle.* You have to put yourself in the way of your dream. If I hadn't bought a saddle, I probably would have eventually gotten a horse anyway. But every time I looked at that saddle, my dream was revitalized. It wasn't long before we got a good deal on a wonderful horse for Vanessa, and I have been a horse owner for the past twenty years. You have to start somewhere.

My dad used to say frequently something like, "We had an opportunity to buy that land, and *we almost bought it.* He would say it with a certain amount of satisfaction as though "almost" was the next best thing to actually doing it. But living in "the land of almost" is a million miles away from significance. You have to take action.

Aging + Strategy + Action = Significance in the Second Half

You simply have to move from the planning stage to the action stage. No matter how great your attitude on aging, no matter how much spiritual maturity you've developed, no matter how perfect your strategy — it only adds up to the *potential* for significance. The plan must be implemented. If you don't begin, you will live in the "land of almost" and never know true significance.

Move forward toward putting your strategy into motion. Here's a quick review of the strategies we covered in the last chapter and some action steps to implement them.

- *Begin to build spiritual health by accepting Christ.*
- *Grow spiritually through church, Bible study, volunteering, consistent prayer, giving of your finances, and witnessing.*

- *Maintain physical health through diet, exercise, health care, and proper mental attitude.*
- *Do your best to strengthen your finances through biblical principles and wise investments.*
- *Identify your goals and vision, and purify your dreams through seeking God's will.*
- *Take the first step in your plan of action.*

Obviously, following through on these strategies can take years. And taking action can be very intimidating and incredibly difficult because inevitably someone (others who are jealous of your vision, negative friends, or Satan) will tell you, "You will *not* succeed. You will fall flat on your face and make a fool of yourself."

It's much safer to stay in your comfort zone. Why take a risk? Because the reward is worth it! Be committed to spiritual health, physical health, and financial health. Be pro-active about implementing your plan, and don't succumb to self-satisfaction or lethargy. Complacency is a rut that is easy to get into and tough to break out of. We are much more vulnerable as we age.

Complacency in the Aging Years

Shirley

Complacency is one of the greatest enemies of significance. It is the opposite of action. The idiom "old and set in his ways" is unfortunately too often true. The dictionary defines complacency as "self-satisfaction, contentment to the point of inactivity, smugness or self-righteousness." Complacency or indifference keeps us in our comfort zone. It's choosing to do the *safe* thing or nothing at all. Pastor Rick Ezell describes it as *sloth,* one of the seven deadly sins. His description is perhaps a bit overstated, but it captures the essence of this unattractive quality at its worst:

"We might call it laziness, apathy, tolerance, or despair. Whatever we call it, it is the sin that believes in nothing, cares for nothing, seeks to know nothing, interferes with nothing, enjoys nothing, loves nothing, hates nothing, finds purpose in nothing and lives for nothing, and it remains alive only because it would die for nothing. It forever remains on the sidelines, unmoved, uncaring, uninvolved."[3]

I, for one, do not want to live my life on the sidelines. Yet, in our older years, it takes more effort to get up and get moving. What are some of the ways we become complacent?

Spiritual complacency can hurt our relationship with God. If we don't grow, we lose ground. It is a hidden sin that can bring coldness where the fires of commitment once burned.

Complacency can cause us to miss God's best. Thirty years ago, Jerry managed a Christian television station for Pat Robertson in Dallas. Jerry loved his job. He often co-hosted the *700 Club* with Pat. Dallas was great; we had close friends; it was Jerry's hometown. Life was good.

After a couple of years, Pat asked Jerry to come to Portsmouth, Virginia, to be operations manager of the entire network. Jerry told him we would pray about it, but everything in us resisted the idea. Even though the move would be a promotion, we didn't want to go to Virginia. We just weren't ready to make a move.

One day, Jerry walked into his office and picked up the phone to make a call. He couldn't see the numbers on the dial and his head was pounding. He couldn't construct a full sentence, and later developed numbness on one side of his body. An EEG procedure revealed an abnormality in the left side of his brain, which was diagnosed as either a stroke or a brain tumor.

There is not room here to tell the complete story of Jerry's journey from panic to supernatural peace, and finally a complete and miraculous healing.[4] But this experience taught us that staying in God's will is more important than homes or friends or the town you live in. Jerry said, "We'll be vagabonds for God for the rest of our lives if that's what God wants." In a few months, we had moved to Virginia.

Did God allow Jerry's illness to shake us out of our lethargy? We believe He did. We did not actively seek God's will about what *He* wanted. God certainly got our attention. It's important to flow with God's divine direction, to move when He says to move, to listen when He speaks, and take action when it's time to act.

Complacency can cause us to stay in a bad situation when we need to make a change. It can cause us to neglect our health and appearance. It can hurt our relationships. We must be pro-active to keep our marriage successful. We must take action to keep family relationships strong and leave a legacy to our grandchildren. Don't let indifference rob you of significance. Take time to build your plan; then take action. The first step is often the hardest. After that, the guidance will be there as you continue to trust God's leading and take the next step in faith.

Use What's in Your Hand

Another reason we fail to act is because we believe we are not adequate for the task. God never asks us to do something we cannot do. You may know that God loves you, but think He has short-changed you in the gifts department. You may think you are not educated enough, or smart enough, or energetic enough to do something really significant. As you plan your strategy, you may feel less and less equipped to pull it off. Thus, you never get to the action.

The Bible is full of people, just like you and me, who God called to perform extremely important tasks. One such person is Moses. He grew up in the home of the powerful ruler of Egypt, the pharaoh. But after killing an Egyptian, he found himself on the back side of the desert in hiding. He lived as a common shepherd for the next forty years — quite a comedown from a prince living in the palace.

When God spoke to Moses and asked him to rescue His people, Moses felt completely inadequate. God asked him to do something very bold, to go to Pharaoh and tell him to free Israel from bondage allowing them to leave Egypt.

Moses said in Exodus 3:11, "Who am I that I should go to Pharaoh?" When Moses argued that Pharaoh would never listen, God said to Moses, "What is that in your hand?" Moses replied, "A rod." But when God told him to throw it down, it became a snake! Moses did exactly what I would have done; he ran away. But when God told him to pick it up, he did. And it became a rod again. God was showing Moses that he held a lot more in his hand than he realized.

Throughout scripture, God uses insignificant people to do great things, using very humble resources. Remember Gideon who proclaimed himself to be the least important member of the poorest family in Israel? God used him to deliver His people with the most unusual weapons — trumpets, pitchers, and lamps (Judges 6). Another example was the little boy who offered Jesus his lunch of five loaves and two fish. Jesus used that little lunch to feed more than five thousand people (Luke 9).

Has God asked you to do something daring? Do you feel ill equipped for the assignment? Maybe you lack education, talent, courage, opportunity. God never asks you to do anything He won't help you do. And, like Moses, God may use what you hold in your hand — some simple gift or talent.

I interviewed Janet (not her real name) who worked for the government but really disliked her job. She was traveling and had a long layover at the airport. Two elderly women waiting in the terminal caught Janet's attention. She decided she would get to know them. She bought ice cream for one of the ladies and chatted with her for awhile. Then Janet began talking to the second lady who was recently widowed. Janet talked with her, offering encouragement to her while they waited. A couple of hours later, after the women had boarded their planes, a third woman approached Janet and said, "I've never done this before. But I just had to tell you, you have the gift of loving people."

Wow! Janet knew she had always enjoyed people. But *the gift of loving people?* She began to think about how she might use that gift to not only bless others but make a living. She resurrected a secret dream she had always had — baking. She made delicious pies and had collected the best recipes over the years. So she decided to open a pie shop. The Sweet Shop was born and has been very successful. She not only serves pies to her customers; she dishes out a generous portion of love. She gives everyone a smile and a hug along with her delicious creations. Happier than she has ever been, she realizes she had the tools she needed all along. Of course, she has worked hard to build her business, taken risks, and had some scary moments. But she is using her gifts to live significantly.

What is that in *your* hand? Is it a love for people? Is it money? Is it musical talent? Is it the tiny hand of a grandchild that you are helping to care for? Is it extra time? Do you have a love for God's Word and Bible teaching? Perhaps you have carpentry skills that could be used on a missions trip. Whatever you have to offer, God can turn it into significance. But you have to take action.

Take Action to Right Wrongs of the Past

Jerry

Have you ever met an older person who is bitter, sour, and disagreeable? One of the saddest ways to grow old is with bitterness. Genuine significance is not possible when we can't get past our past.

There's a Spanish story of a father and son who had become estranged. The son ran away, and the father set off to find him. He searched for months to no avail. Finally, in a last desperate effort to find his son, the father put an ad in a Madrid newspaper. The ad read:

Dear Paco. Meet me in front of this newspaper office at noon on Saturday. All is forgiven. I love you. Your Father

On Saturday eight hundred Pacos showed up, looking for forgiveness and love from their fathers! (sermonillustrations.com)

Holding onto bitterness, unforgiveness, anger, and grudges is not only bad for your health, it can bring on premature aging and even cause death.

William H. Walton once said, "To carry a grudge is like being stung to death by one bee." One hurtful incident can stick with someone for decades causing unhappiness, illness, emotional problems, and even an early demise. I have seen families torn apart by disagreements over one valueless item of an inheritance. I know siblings who have not spoken for years because of petty jealousy and misunderstandings. I know fathers and children who have been estranged for decades because they just can't let go of grudges. That is no way to live and certainly no way to grow old.

Jesus tells us, "So if you are standing before the altar in the Temple, offering a sacrifice to God, and suddenly remember that a friend has something against you, leave your sacrifice there beside the altar and go and apologize and be reconciled to him, and then come and offer your sacrifice to God." (Matthew 5: 23, 24 (TLB) Why do you suppose Jesus chose the setting of standing in church, getting ready to offer a gift to the Lord? Because any gift you offer to God is only meaningful if your heart is right. If you are holding onto bitterness against someone, or if someone else has a reason to be upset with you, then your heart is not right and your gift will not be accepted. Taking action to right wrongs of the past is critical to living significantly. As long as you are harboring ill will, you will never know the true joy, purpose, and fulfillment God wants for you. If you are the one that's been wronged, it takes determination and spiritual maturity to let go of past hurts.

Corrie ten Boom, a Dutch woman imprisoned in a Nazi concentration camp during World War II, had a lot of forgiving to do when the war was over. She survived the nightmare of Nazi persecution, witnessing friends and family being murdered. She watched her dear sister Betsy die in the concentration camp. But there was such a need for forgiveness in post-war Europe, Corrie felt called by God to travel across the continent with a message of forgiveness.

She tells the story of a service in Munich where she was approached by a member of her appreciative audience. "Miss ten Boom," the man said, "I am so glad that Jesus forgives us all for our sins, as you say." He reached to shake her hand. Instantly, Corrie recognized him as a former German soldier, one of the guards who used to leer at and taunt the women prisoners in the work camps as they showered together. She could not shake his hand. All at once, she found herself unable to forgive. She had been so sure that through the power of Jesus she had overcome all the pain of the past. Now the hate was as strong as it had ever been. She didn't know what to do. So in her heart, she cried out, "Jesus, I can't forgive this man. Please forgive me."

As she prayed, Corrie felt relieved of the hatred. She knew the Lord had forgiven her and that she could forgive him. In the power of that knowledge, she reached out and took the hand of her former enemy. Corrie was freed from the burden of her own unforgiving spirit, just as the soldier had been freed from his past sins.

Sometimes it seems that we have been wronged too badly, hurt too deeply to forgive. In those cases, just like Corrie, we need to seek God's help to do what seems impossible.

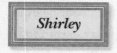

Shirley

I interviewed Jan Coates whose only son Chris had been killed by a drunk driver. At the trial, the man showed no remorse. In fact, in the hallway outside the courtroom, he spit in Jan's face. To make matters worse, the judge just gave him a slap on his wrist and two months probation.

Though a new Christian, Jan was so overwhelmed with bitterness and anger at the man that she actually tried to buy a gun with the intent of taking his life. Eventually, she got past her hatred and knew she needed to forgive him, but just couldn't. God told her, "I know you can't forgive him right now, so give it to Me. I can forgive him." In time, Jan *could* forgive him and pray for him. If she hadn't gotten past her bitterness, she would not be the happy, loving mother of two that she is today.

A rattlesnake, if cornered, will sometimes become so angry it will bite itself.

That is exactly what the harboring of hate and resentment against others is — a biting of oneself. We think we are harming others by holding onto these spites and hates, but the deeper harm is to ourselves. (E. Stanley Jones, *Reader's Digest*, December 1981)

Bruce Goodrich was being initiated into the cadet corps at Texas A & M University. One night, Bruce was forced to run until he dropped — but he never got up. Bruce Goodrich died before he even entered college.

A short time after the tragedy, Bruce's father wrote this letter to the administration, faculty, student body, and the corps of cadets:

> "*I would like to take this opportunity to express the appreciation of my family for the great outpouring of concern and sympathy from Texas A & M University and the college community over the loss of our son Bruce. We were deeply touched by the tribute paid to him in the battalion. We were particularly pleased to note that his Christian witness did not go unnoticed during his brief time on campus. I hope it will be some comfort to know that we harbor no ill will in the matter. We know our God makes no mistakes. Bruce had an appointment with his Lord and is now secure in his celestial home. When the question is asked, 'Why did this happen?' perhaps one answer will be, 'So that many will consider where they will spend eternity.'*" (*Our Daily Bread*, March 22, 1994)

What an example of grace and forgiveness being given where some would say it wasn't deserved. Of course, the stellar example for all of us is Jesus's own forgiveness of his executioners. He said, "Father, forgive them for they know not what they do." In an even greater act of love, Jesus forgave us all of our sins — generations past and generations to come. He took all the sin that belonged to us, paid the price for it, and set us free. There is no greater demonstration of forgiveness.

How do you go about re-building shattered relationships? It starts with action. Sit down and write the person who has hurt you. Let him or her know that you're over it and regret the estrangement. Be careful not to be accusatory; you don't have to include all the details. Say something like, "This has come between us long enough. I want to make things right." Express that you sincerely want to put it behind you. Then send the letter or email, and pray about the situation. If you don't get a response, wait a few weeks and try again. It is well worth whatever effort it takes to start the healing process. Even if the parties involved have passed away, or no contact is possible, write your letter anyway. The action will be healing for you. Then move on knowing that your heart is right with God.

Take Action to Forgive Yourself

Sometimes it is harder to forgive ourselves than it is to forgive others. You may know that you are the one who has caused all the pain and division, broken relationships, and missed opportunities. The longer we carry that burden and the older we get, the more difficult it is to forgive ourselves. Of course, the first step is to confess it to God and ask His forgiveness. Once He has forgiven you, move toward forgiving yourself. You cannot have fruitful aging years if you live under a burden of past sins and mistakes.

Here's Paul's profound advice, "Forgetting those things which are behind," he declared, "and reaching forth unto those things which are before, I press toward the mark for the prize of the high calling of God in Christ Jesus." (Philippians 3:13-14) Paul had persecuted and killed Christians. He had held the coats of the men who had stoned Stephen to death. He had fought directly against the Savior he eventually came to serve. He had to forgive himself.

Karl Menninger, the famed psychiatrist, once said that if he could convince the patients in psychiatric hospitals that their sins were forgiven, seventy-five percent of them could walk out the next day! (*Today in the Word*, March, 1989) Aren't you glad that whatever we have done, Christ has forgiven us and provided for a restored relationship with God? We just have to accept it and forgive ourselves.

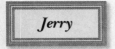

A friend of mine I'll call John was a very successful pastor, well known and respected in the large city where he served. But a serious moral failure broke up his family, ruined his ministry and his reputation, and nearly destroyed his church. He struggled under the weight of guilt and failure — and eventually he came to the conclusion that his sin was too great for God to forgive. For years, he lived under this horrible cloud of divine rejection. Ironically, it was in Egypt that God delivered John from his spiritual bondage — the same place he had delivered the Israelites.

John and I were in Egypt on a tour, along with Steve Freed, the son of Paul Freed, founder of Trans World Radio. One evening after dinner, Steve fell ill from food poisoning. He was soon dehydrated to the point that his life was in danger. John was the only one with Steve that evening, and in desperation he fell to his knees beside Steve's hotel bed and cried out to God for his life.

Within minutes, Steve began to experience a remarkable recovery. When the Egyptian doctor arrived, he was surprised at Steve's recovery — confirming that this young man had only been a few minutes from death. For years afterward, every time I was with Paul Freed, he would tell the story of how John's prayers had saved his son's life.

However, it was John who was most profoundly affected by the incident. When Steve was miraculously healed, John realized that God had actually heard his prayer! God still loved him and had forgiven him. For all those years, in John's spiritual wilderness, God had never been farther than a prayer away. He was waiting for John to call on Him, just like the Israelites. God's love for John had never changed — even when he sinned. The unbearable weight of guilt was lifted, and John's relationship with Christ was restored.

Shirley

None of us who have lived 50 years or more can say we haven't made mistakes. Life presents years of opportunities to fail. Sometimes we just do stupid things. We make bad choices and hurt people either on purpose or accidentally. But God forgives and forgets (Isaiah 43:25). And we can take action to right the wrongs. If you're dealing with guilt and feelings of unworthiness, it's the devil's deception. He knows you have the potential for significance and that God is just waiting to plug you in! There is a perfect example in the Old Testament of an unlikely little orphan girl who felt totally inadequate, but she stepped from obscurity into greatness.

Esther Acts to Save Her People

Perhaps the most beloved of all the women in the Bible is Queen Esther. She had been brought to the palace of the powerful king of Persia. She competed in the most famous beauty contest in history and won. She was chosen to be the new queen.

Esther was not a woman of royal birth. She was "queen" of the harem — the reigning favorite wife at the time. Esther's exalted status did, however, allow her certain privileges. As "queen consort," she was allowed to wear the royal tiara and was the acknowledged head of the female apartments. The other concubines honored her by actual prostration. She had great wealth of her own, not necessarily by the will of the king, but by Persian law. She now wore the splendid attire and extravagant ornamentation of the queen of Persia.[5] Lovely little Esther had come a long way from her cousin Mordecai's humble home. She had become very comfortable and accustomed to the luxury of the women's apartments.

When the villain Haman enters the picture, threatening to annihilate the entire Hebrew race, Mordecai put on the sackcloth and ashes of mourning. Then he went to Esther for help. She had been chosen as queen and had the opportunity

128

to stand in the gap for her people. He asked his cousin to go to the king and appeal for their lives.

Esther wasn't so sure. She knew the law. You didn't just go marching into the king's chambers anytime you wanted. Unless you were summoned, it could mean your immediate execution. Queen or not, Esther wasn't so sure anymore about where she stood with King Xerxes. He hadn't called for her in over a month.

Then Mordecai got practical. He gave his newly exalted cousin a wake-up call. "Think not that in the king's palace you will escape any more than all the other Jews." (4:13)

If Esther refused to take the risk, it could have cost *her* life and many others as well. But Esther *did* take the risk. She not only had a brilliant strategy, she was willing to take that first terrifying step to put her plan into action. She demonstrated outstanding courage to appeal to the king for her people. She used cunning, wisdom, and a great sense of timing to make it happen. She was incredibly successful. The Hebrew race was saved and Esther found her way into Jewish history.

Do you have a deep desire to do something for the Kingdom? But just find yourself too timid, or unprepared, or just too comfortable to take that first step? It's interesting to note Esther's steps to accomplishing her mission — steps we can emulate to start living significantly.

Esther's Steps to Significance

1. She overcame her fear. Esther knew her life was in danger, but she had to face her fear and overcome it. So must we, in order to take action toward significance. The first way to overcome your fear is to identify it. What are you really afraid of? Are you afraid of appearing foolish? Are you afraid of criticism, afraid of failure? Is your pride getting in the way of courage? Giving a name to your fear is a good way to put it into perspective. Prayer and meditating on God's promises can also help to alleviate your fears. Scriptures such as this one in Hebrews 13:5, 6 are great faith builders: God has said, "… I will never, never fail you nor forsake you." That is why we can say without any doubt or fear, "The lord is my helper and I am not afraid of anything that mere men can do to me." (TLB) Also consider Psalms 34:4, 2 Timothy 1:7, and Luke 12:7.

One way I have overcome fear is to go ahead and imagine the worst thing that could happen. Then I symbolically give that situation to God, knowing that nothing is impossible with Him and knowing He has promised to help me and make all things work together for my good.

You may never be asked to save a whole race of people. But sooner or later, God will ask each of us to do something radical, or at least something that shoves us way out of our comfort zone. "Radical" for some may be standing in front of others to speak or teach. "Radical" for another may be traveling to foreign lands to give of their time and talents. It may be starting a business or a ministry. True courage means moving forward in obedience — in spite of your fear.

2. *She had a submissive spirit.* I don't know if Esther was given a choice about entering the beauty contest, but she went willingly. She submitted herself to Mordecai and went along with the year-long preparations, and then later submitted to the role of Xerxes' wife. When her cousin asked her to appeal to the king, she finally agreed. Submission and obedience don't come naturally for most of us. God may ask you to do something you've never done before. You may have spent a career as head of your company, and now you are asked to fill a servant's role. Paul says: "Honor Christ by submitting to each other."(Ephesians 5:21) (TLB) Whatever we do in Christ's name is important and significant. Ask God to give you a submissive spirit. That doesn't mean you are weak; it means you have a cooperative attitude, a teachable spirit, and the courage to take action, even when the future is unsure.

3. *She sought divine guidance and help from others.* Once Esther decided to move ahead with the dangerous plan, she knew

she needed help. Perhaps the most important step she took was to seek divine help and support from others. She asked all the Jews to fast and pray for three days, and she did the same. If only we could grasp the importance of dependency on God. We live in a society that prides itself on being independent. We view dependency as a weak and ugly trait. But throughout the Bible, God asked the least likely people to carry out the important missions because He knew they would have to depend on Him. Gideon, Moses, and Jesus's mother Mary are examples of some who were inadequate, but with God's help accomplished the impossible. Esther knew the importance of prayer support. Never hesitate to ask others to pray for you. When God asks you to step into a risky situation, He will equip you and empower you. But He wants you to admit your inadequacy for the task and rely on Him to accomplish it.

4. *She was sensitive to God's timing.* When we are reluctant to activate the plan God has given us, we often miss God's timing by dragging our feet and not obeying quickly enough. On the other hand, sometimes we can get ahead of God. Esther's story shows us that the secret to moving in God's timetable is earnest prayer, patience, and listening to the wise counsel of others as well as the still, small voice of the Lord. When that voice says, "Go," then move forward with courage.

In summary, as we age it's easy to become complacent. What can we do to get going? First, listen to God and respond to what He's telling you. Second, believe in your calling enough to do something tangible. (If you want a horse, buy a saddle.) Third, use whatever God has put in your hands, rather than focusing on what you *don't* have. Fourth, and perhaps the most difficult, right the wrongs of the past. Forgive others who have hurt you and forgive yourself. Then step out in faith, and be courageous. Like Esther, God will use you to do something significant. But, remember that every journey begins with a first step.

Action Steps to Implement Your Strategy:

• *Resist complacency and be obedient to your calling.*

• *Do something tangible (put yourself in the way of your dream).*

• *Follow through with your plan to strengthen your spiritual, physical, and financial health.*

• *Focus on using what resources, gifts, and talents, you have, and don't focus on what you don't have.*

• *Right wrongs of the past; forgive others and yourself. Step out in courage and faith to implement your plan for significance.*

Suggested Reading

Discovering your Divine Assignment, Robin Chaddock

Putting Your Past Behind You, Erwin W. Lutzer

Spiritual Seasons, Thomas A. Vaughn

This Day We Fight, Francis Frangipane

Aging Prayer

Lord, you know better than I know myself that I'm growing older.
Keep me from getting too talkative,
and thinking I must say something on every subject and on every occasion.
Release me from craving to straighten out everybody's affairs.
Teach me the glorious lesson that occasionally it is possible that
I may be mistaken.
Make me thoughtful, but not moody;
helpful, but not bossy;
For You know, Lord, that I want a few friends at the end.

Grandchildren

A little boy opened the big family bible. He was fascinated as he fingered the old pages. Suddenly, something fell out. It was an old leaf that had been pressed between the pages. "Grandpa, look what I found," he called out. "What have you got there, sonny?" With wonder in his voice he answered, "I think it's Adam's underwear."

My grandson got lost at the health club and found himself in the women's locker room. When he was spotted, the room burst into shrieks, with ladies grabbing towels and running for cover. The little guy watched in amazement and then asked, "What's the matter? Haven't you ever seen a little boy before?"

While working for an organization that delivers lunches to the elderly, I used to take my 4-year-old granddaughter on my route. The various appliances of old age, particularly the canes, walkers, and wheelchairs intrigued her. One day I found her staring at a pair of false teeth soaking in a glass. As I braced myself for the inevitable questions, she merely turned and whispered, "The tooth fairy will never believe this!"

Sixth Coordinate:
Connection
Don't Go it Alone

*And they continued steadfastly in…fellowship,
and in breaking of bread, and of prayers.*

Acts 2:42

Shirley

Having grown up near New Orleans, I watched CNN in horror as Katrina decimated my hometown. I had been through hurricanes many times during my youth, and once we had flood waters damage our home. But Katrina was different. This time the water came in a twenty-foot storm surge that rushed in like a Tsunami. It washed away homes and drowned dozens of people. Unlike previous floods, the water reached the rooftops and stayed there for weeks.

My sister Esther and her husband Ronnie still lived in the town of Chalmette where I grew up. They had both recently retired, their home was paid for, and they were looking forward to more time to spend in ministry and volunteer work. They had evacuated to Houston, and, a few days after the storm, they saw a satellite photo of their home. The flood waters were up to the peak of their roof. They realized they would never be going home.

I have never been more proud of my sister. She and Ronnie (like so many others) lost everything — their furnishings, clothes, books, photos, and all the things that made up their lives and memories. But they faced their loss with amazing peace and a positive attitude. Esther said, "I couldn't bring myself to cry over things. I had my faith in God, and I had my family. That is all that matters."

Esther and Ronnie eventually got a meager settlement from their insurance company and were faced with the decision of where to settle. There was no possibility of going back to their old neighborhood. Now, a year after Katrina, many of the homes in that area have been demolished, my sister's included. Like some of the other low-lying areas, it may simply be reclaimed by the waters of southeastern Louisiana. So the question loomed, *where could they settle and rebuild their lives?*

I certainly wanted them well away from New Orleans and out of harm's way. Esther's children wanted them to move to Texas or Arizona where they had family. Esther and Ronnie considered all these possibilities, but ultimately settled an hour north of New Orleans. While they are not in a low-lying area like their old neighborhood, they are still close to the coast — in hurricane alley. Why would Esther and Ronnie choose to live so close to the danger zone? They no longer have jobs that demand they stay in the area. Why take a chance?

Like many Americans in their sixties, community and friends are very important to them. When it actually came down to moving away, they chose to take a chance on future hurricanes rather than give up their church, friends, and the culture they had always known. Each Saturday, they go back to Chalmette to volunteer at a center that helps the victims of Katrina. They give out food, clothing, furniture, prayers, and encouragement. On Sunday morning, they often drive over an hour to be with their small church group. Though they lost all their material possessions, they just could not bring themselves to give up their human connections.

Independence vs. Community

A core value in America is to live independently. America fought for its independence and celebrates it every Fourth of July. We have come to believe we can "make it on our own." We have our 401k's and try to invest wisely so we can be financially independent. Those things are important, but it is a mistake to think independence brings happiness. The fact is, just the opposite is true. Happiness comes when we live connected with others.[1]

Boomers are beginning to realize the value of being connected. They were driven to get more education, make money, and keep moving up the corporate ladder. Consequently, they became mobile and had five to ten jobs during their working years. But now that they are approaching retirement, they long for a re-connection with their roots, their family, and their friends.

This longing for connection and community explains the success of retirement communities like Sun City, Arizona. Yes, there is low crime, light traffic, low- maintenance lawns, plenty of recreation, and low stress. But another attraction is the opportunity to be involved in others' lives. One of Sun City's residents, James Nordstrom, aged seventy-three, says:

I love my wife more than anything ... I've read the statistics. I know that I'll probably die before she does. When that happens, I intend to leave this life knowing that during her remaining years she will never feel isolated and helpless and without supportive and available friends ... if she was

*stuck all alone in an apartment in the city…she'd never have the
opportunity she has here …*[2]

And yet many still live their lives in isolation. This is especially true in large cities.
I spent a year helping an older gentleman who I'll call Charlie. He had lived in
the heart of Chicago for about thirty years, all alone in a small studio apartment.
Charlie had no relatives or friends in the city.

As he grew older, he was less able to take care of himself, so he contacted
our ministry, and I was asked to help him. I was astounded at his lifestyle. He
had very little interaction with other people. His apartment door had at least six
locks, and yet he was absolutely certain someone was entering his home and
pilfering his belongings.

Charlie was distrustful of his neighbors, afraid for his health, and was certain
that his phone was tapped. Having no cell phone, he would walk blocks in the
snow and cold to call on a pay phone because he didn't think he could speak
freely in his home.

I succeeded in finding a retirement center that he seemed to like and
could easily afford. So we signed him up and moved him in. The people and
surroundings were pleasant. There were a lot of activities for the residents,
and it was located in a lovely, safe neighborhood in the suburbs. I thought
Charlie would be happy there.

Everything went okay for the first few weeks. Then I learned that Charlie
was staying in his room more often and was frequently missing meals. Finally,
he told me he suspected that people were coming into his room and stealing his
medication. Though potential friends were all around him, his mistrust and fear
kept him isolated. We moved Charlie to Michigan to be with his niece, praying
he would be at peace.

You're probably thinking he was just a crazy old man. But Charlie was
only seventy-four and very sharp mentally. His paranoia came from all those years of
seclusion. He was afraid to make friends; he distrusted others and pushed them away.

We live in a day when especially men suffer from isolation and lack of
connection. With the rise in divorce and abandonment by their fathers, men lack

the blessing and involvement of their dads, and it affects them emotionally.
Many men are living in quiet desperation, longing for intimate relationships,
but insecure and afraid to make themselves vulnerable.

Relationships are risky, but we're wired by God to be connected and
dependent on others. We're not built for isolation. We're built for community.
I love 1 Peter 3:8 in the Living Bible: "And now this word to all of you:
you should be like one big happy family, full of sympathy toward each
other, loving one another with tender hearts and humble minds."

The Need to be Loved

Jerry

When I was a young man, I learned a profound lesson in the value of caring
for people and how much they need love. I worked as a disk jockey for KMAP-
FM in Dallas. I was still single, so the crazy hours and madcap workload suited me
perfectly. I worked every shift possible and learned everything I could about radio.
Eventually, I was able to host a mellow, late night sign-off show called *Lovers
and Losers*. It featured slow, easy jazz — perfect for putting people to sleep.

One night as I was about to conclude the program, I opened the mike and
spoke softly to my audience. "Okay, you night-owls, it's time to go to bed. You
just kick back now and relax while I put you to sleep with some easy-listening
music." I got an idea to go a little further.

"Say, why don't you set your alarm about five minutes later than usual?"
I suggested quietly, warmly. I pictured a listener — female, living alone. "Give
yourself some extra time to sleep in." I went on in a rambling, lazy, sleepy voice.
"And hey, by the way, have you checked the door? You know better than to go
to bed and leave your door unlocked. Check it out ... that's right. Now lay out
the red dress. You look really nice in that red dress."

Like a friendly, intimate soul mate, I added, "Now just snuggle under
those covers while I play you some gentle jazz."

Then I punched in the song — instantly the switchboard lit up in a blaze! Calls came from women all over Dallas. I got invitations to breakfast, lunch, dinner, and otherwise. It was as if I had broken some emotional dam. Many called to tell me their problems. You would have thought I was a psychologist — or an intimate friend.

At first I was dumbfounded, but soon I realized what had happened. Lonely women of all ages and backgrounds needed someone to care about them. The sound of my voice, the concern I expressed for their safety and comfort appealed to them. My caring, even if it arose out of an electronic box, came as a rare and unique gift to brighten their sad, empty lives. They called because they thought maybe, just maybe, the man on the radio really was concerned about their loneliness, their hurt, their insecurities.

As I signed off the air that night, the experience hung in my mind like a heavy mist that would not evaporate. Three distinct impressions came out of the mist. First, I saw people's desperate need for someone to care about them. Second, I was jolted by the power I seemed to have over these women because of my position in the media. If I had not really cared — if I had been irresponsible and callused — I could have accepted some of their offers, exploited them, and abused their trust. I had seen plenty of radio and television personalities do just that. And third, I realized the power of the media and how it could be used to meet people's needs. With its national and even international reach, a television or radio station could broadcast a message of hope, love, and forgiveness to desperately hurting people without fear of exploitation or abuse. They could call in to the station, and caring people would be there to listen to them, pray for them, and show them a path to hope and faith.

It would be years before I would work in Christian television, but that experience shaped my perspective on TV as a ministry. It laid the foundation for a telephone prayer ministry that became a vital part of TV38 and TLN years later. We would not be isolated from the viewers. We would be interactive. And our telephone volunteers would be called our "Careforce." Because everyone needs someone to care.

The Healing Power of Intimacy

You may recognize the name of Dean Ormish, the doctor who proved symptoms of heart disease can be reversed with a regimen of a low-fat diet, exercise, and stress reduction. In his new book *Love and Survival,* he shows how dozens of scientific studies have demonstrated that personal intimacy is as important to our physical condition as to our mental health. Ormish states that more than diet, exercise, stress, genetics, smoking, or surgery, the greatest influence on healing is being connected to others in a loving, intimate way. This love and intimacy has more of an impact on our quality of life, incidence of illness, and premature death than any other factor. (Amazon.com, Editorial Reviews Kirkus Reviews)

Leonard Syme, a professor of epidemiology at the University of California at Berkeley, indicates the importance of social ties and social support systems in relationship to mortality and disease rates. He points to Japan as the healthiest country in the world, and it's not because the Japanese eat all that tofu. He believes it's the close social, cultural, and traditional ties of the population. The closer the social ties, the better the health and the lower the death rate. Conversely, the more isolated the person, the poorer the health and the higher the death rate.[3]

Is it any wonder that isolated, lonely people like Charlie are plagued with numerous health problems? Connection and interdependence with others are fundamental building blocks for physical health, and connection is an important key to significance.

Why We Need Others

Shirley

I have sung in choirs most of my life. There is nothing like choir music. To me, no soloist alive, no matter how talented, can come close to the powerful music that pours from a choir singing as one in perfect harmony. Symphony orchestras, made up of a hundred separate instruments, can create a melody no single instrument can. Likewise, though there are many things we can do alone, our impact can be multiplied many times over when we join together with other Christians seeking to be used by God.

God never intended for us to go through life alone. Someone has said, "A burden shared is half a burden; a joy shared is twice the joy!" Usually it takes connection and community to fulfill God's plan for our lives. I recently heard a pastor point out some important reasons we need others.[4]

1. We need others to walk with us. The Christian life is a journey, a walk. (Colossians 2:6) God never intended for us to walk alone. This is true for singles, those widowed, as well as married people. Some married people are the loneliest.

Have you ever been in a huge crowd, but felt utterly alone? Unfortunately, people feel this way in some of our large churches. A church is a good place to find a community. But a church is not necessarily a community — it's a crowd. Real community is an intimate group of people who are like minded, who love God together, and serve together. How can we fulfill 1 Corinthians 13, the scripture that describes real, sacrificial love, if we are not close to others to demonstrate it? That's why, especially in large churches, small groups are so important. We need the connection, the opportunity to help each other, and the accountability of close friendships. **Community is God's answer to loneliness.**

Sometimes a caring group of Christian friends can provide a better community than even your own family. Family members die, move away, and grow apart. But your spiritual family is eternal. You will have fellowship with them all the days of your life, and then continue that fellowship in heaven.

There is *safety* in numbers. Have you ever walked down a dark alley and wished you had someone with you? There are places I won't walk alone. But if I have someone with me, I feel safe, and, in a group, I feel even safer.

There is *support* when we walk with others. Friends offer encouragement and wisdom when you are discouraged. They can give you a whole new perspective — especially if they have walked through the same trial. When you run alone, you can run *faster*; but when you run with others, you can run *farther*. Geese fly in a V formation because the aerodynamics allow them to fly farther and expend less energy than they could alone. The same principle applies to our life journey.

141

It's also *smarter* to walk with others. We might pride ourselves in our self-sufficiency, but it is wiser to take advantage of the knowledge and experiences of others. We should never hesitate to ask for help or advice when we need it. Proverbs 12:15 says, "A fool thinks he needs no advice, but a wise man listens to others." (TLB) Collective wisdom is a huge benefit of community.

2. *We need others to work with us.* Ephesians 2:10 says we are "created in Christ Jesus unto good works." God intends for all of us to work. You cannot achieve significance without effort. You can give large amounts of money to good causes, and perhaps that is one of your callings. But writing checks is not the same as rolling up your sleeves and getting involved in something significant.

So much more can be accomplished for the Kingdom when we work together. Whether it's running a successful church, putting on a women's conference, conducting Vacation Bible School, or reaching out to your community, it's nearly impossible to go solo. We are often exhausted and burned out because we try to go it alone. **Community is God's answer to fatigue.**

3. *We need others to witness with us.* Sharing our faith can be scary. But when we join together with others, it is less intimidating, more effective, and even more enjoyable. I can remember as a teenager gathering with others from my youth group to witness at a park in our neighborhood. Because we were all in it together, we had the courage to approach people with the gospel message. We saw people come to Christ every time. **Community is God's answer to fear and intimidation.**

I recently took some friends to a large women's conference here in Chicago. As I sat in that huge crowd of fifteen thousand women, I was awe struck. I tried to imagine just how many people it took to bring about a conference of this magnitude. There were about eight speakers, music groups, video and sound people, marketing teams, ticket sellers, instrumentalists, worship teams, and prayer counselors among many others. It took literally an army of staff and volunteers to pull it off. But it was phenomenal — well worth the effort. My friends and I (and thousands of others) got a generous portion of fun, entertainment, spiritual teaching, ministry, stirring personal testimonies, and a clear message of the gospel. No one person could ever equal that kind of impact.

4. We need others to watch out for us. Who's got your back? In this day and age, strong friendships are not so common, especially among men. Women seem to have a greater need for connection; men learn from an early age to be self-sufficient. My husband is a good example. He is just a naturally private person. Having had a very "public" ministry for decades, he values privacy and anonymity. He has to make a real effort to cultivate friendships. But I encourage him, because it is so important to have friends in our lives to watch out for us. Sometimes it's just difficult to find friends who we can trust with the private part of our lives.

It reminds me of the story of the three pastors who decided they needed to forge closer friendships with one another, so they planned a fishing trip together. Out on the lake by themselves, they began to open up. They felt it would be good for their souls to share their most guarded secrets with these other men of God.

The first preacher admitted that his worst fault was that he loved alcohol. He had kept it hidden from his family and his congregation, but he had a drinking problem. The other two men were very sympathetic and promised to pray for him.

The second pastor shared his darkest secret. He admitted that he had a problem with women. He had cheated on his wife and had affairs with women in the congregation. Though he struggled to be free, he just couldn't curb his lust. The other two pastors were very sympathetic and assured him they would pray for him.

When it was the third preacher's turn, he sheepishly admitted to the other two men that he only had one fault. He said, "My one sin is that I can't keep a secret. I blab everything I hear!"

Unfortunately, I think, we've all had a friend like that who causes us to isolate ourselves to avoid vulnerability. Don't be that kind of friend. Speak the truth in love. Be honest. Pray for one another. But never betray confidences!

Do you have friends who can be painfully honest with you? We have seen devastating moral failures in the lives of major spiritual leaders. One of them encapsulated the problem when he asked, "Who could I go to?" Accountability is one very important reason for close connections. **Community is God's answer to failure and defeat.**

5. We need others to weep with us. We will all experience trials and heartache, especially as we get older. Advice columnist Abigail Van Buren once said, "The deepest definition of youth is life yet untouched by tragedy." At our age, we can expect to lose loved ones, face illness, have problems with our children, or *something*. In these times of crisis, it is more important than ever to be connected to Christian friends. None of us should have to face funerals, divorce courts, hospitals, or serious diagnoses by ourselves.

But if you don't invest in others, you will likely face these trials alone. It takes time and effort to develop friendships, but the fellowship, support, and love you receive are well worth it. **Community is God's answer to despair.**

How Can We Stay Connected?

With Our Spouse

We have already discussed the importance of being pro-active and consistent about building your marriage relationship. Midlife can either bring husbands and wives closer, or it can be deadly to the marriage. It is estimated that couples over sixty have more than a thirty percent chance of divorcing before one of the partners dies.

Jerry and I have completely enjoyed the empty nest. Even though we both tend to be workaholics, we do have more time to spend together. We have enjoyed going out to eat whenever the notion strikes us. We have more time to talk. We can pop in a video or turn on a television show because no one is monopolizing the set. We can travel together whenever the opportunity arises. It's been fun.

We are enjoying our newfound freedom. But that same freedom allows us to go flying off in opposite directions. With no demands from other family members, we tend to work even more. After dinner, it's normal for Jerry to head down the hallway to his home office and for me to bee-line it upstairs to my study where we work until late in the evening.

We don't have a lot of hobbies in common, so weekends also found us doing our own thing. We finally realized the empty nest had not brought us closer, but driven us farther apart. We couldn't blame anyone but ourselves for the distance between us. So we sat down and had a heart-to-heart. We agreed we would make our relationship a priority. We would use this time of transition to grow our marriage and make it better than ever. We would be faithful about having date nights and quality time together.

The empty nest can offer more focused time for each other, more privacy, and renewed intimacy. Plan a time each day for meaningful conversation, times to go out to do something fun. Have extended times together when true intimacy and soul connection can take place. And very importantly, plan sex dates. Whatever it takes, stay connected to your mate.

With Adult Children

We've all heard, "You can pick your friends, but not your family." Community certainly starts at home, but the second half of life brings the empty nest, and geography often separates us from our loved ones. Ours is a mobile society. Unlike years ago, when families stayed in the same neighborhood or rural area for generations, it is rare to find an entire extended family living in close proximity. Even if you are fortunate enough to have your children, grandchildren, parents, and siblings nearby, proximity doesn't equal closeness. One thing is certain as parents; you have to love unconditionally, be tough-skinned, and be diligent about staying connected.

Nancy Heche, mother of the actress Ann Heche, described on our television program the pain she experienced when she heard that Ann was in a relationship with Ellen DeGeneres. Ann hurt her mother time and time again by the things she said, sometimes on national TV. She and Nancy would have horrible fights on the phone. They would go for a year or more without speaking.

Once when Nancy was flying, she was thinking about Ann and how heartbroken she was about her behavior. God spoke to Nancy and said, "You need to bless her right where she is."

It was such a strong impression, that, when Nancy landed, she called Ann and told her, "Ann, I bless you. I don't agree with all you are doing, but I love you, and I bless you."

It was the beginning of healing for their fractured relationship. It was not long before Ann and Ellen had broken up. Nancy has continued to love Ann and make an effort to be a part of her life. Though she often disapproves of her lifestyle, she still loves her daughter.

We know the harm that comes from bitterness and how difficult it is to right wrongs of the past. The best policy is to never let the bitterness take root in the first place. Be forgiving and learn to let the hurts roll off. Accept one another — the good, the bad, and the ugly — and don't expect perfection. The test of true friendship, true commitment, and true community is to love in the bad times as well as the good.

Be proactive in your children's lives. If you have to initiate the contact, make the first phone call, so be it. There is a delicate balance between staying connected and not being a nuisance. Talk with your kids honestly. Ask them to suggest a good time for you to phone them. Be together as much as you can, but be sensitive to their schedules. Don't interfere, but do everything you can to be a part of their lives. There is no greater blessing in your aging years than to have your adult children as your best friends. However, it's a delicate dance. It takes practice and some blunders and a lot of prayer. But keep communication open, and let your kids know you want a relationship with them and that you are there for them. As they mature, and you learn from your mistakes, chances are you can have the relationship you've always wanted.

With Grandchildren

An eight-year-old wrote, "A grandmother is a lady who has no children of her own, so she likes other people's boys and girls. Grandmas don't have anything to do except be there. They wear glasses, and sometimes they can take their teeth out. When they read to us, they don't skip words or mind if it is the same story again. Everybody should try to have a grandma, especially if you don't have television, because grandmas are the only grownups who always have time." (Unknown)

I've been a grandmother for eleven years now, and I've always considered it a second chance at parenting. How many times when my children were little did I not have time for them? How often, through selfishness or busy-ness, did I miss a treasure right under my nose? We all make mistakes as parents, and we cannot dwell on them; but I try to do a much better job at being a grandparent. For me, grandchildren have been the best part of aging.

How do we stay connected with those little ones, especially if they live away? I cannot understand how grandparents would *choose* to be disconnected, but apparently that happens. Research, based on interviews with children and grandparents, shows that children need their grandparents and vice-versa. That bond is second in emotional power and influence only to the relationship between parents and children. Of the children studied, only five percent reported close, regular contact with at least one grandparent. When the grandparents choose to remain emotionally distant, the children appear to be hurt and angry. One of them said, "I'm just a charm on grandma's bracelet."

When a child has a strong emotional tie to a grandparent, he enjoys a kind of immunity — he doesn't have to perform the way he must for his parents, peers, and teachers. The love of grandparents comes with no behavioral strings attached. (*Youthletter*, September, 1981)

If we don't make an effort to be a part of our grandkids' lives, we miss perhaps our greatest opportunity to be an influencer.

With Friends and Relatives

George Eliot wrote:

Oh, the comfort, the inexpressible comfort of feeling safe with a person, having neither to weigh thoughts, nor measure words, but to pour them all out just as they are, chaff and grain together knowing that a faithful hand will take and sift them, keep what is worth keeping, and then, with the breath of kindness blow the rest away. [5]

What a beautiful description of friendship.

The past few years, I have felt a growing need to re-connect with friends and relatives with whom I've lost touch. Maybe it's my age, or it could just be the convenience of email, but I have re-established relationships with cousins I hadn't spoken to in years. My lack of communication was not intentional.

147

Our lives are just so busy. As we age, we can become complacent about keeping friendships alive and flourishing.

I heard the true story of two couples who were the best of friends. Bennett and Mildred and Woodrow and Betty lived in the same town. They had many things in common and were very close. They vacationed in Europe together and spent every summer in Tahoe.

As they got older, Woodrow's wife Betty passed away, and the other couple moved a hundred and fifty miles away to be with family. Over time, they just stopped communicating. In just a few years, the friendship had deteriorated to the point that Woodrow wasn't sure he even cared to attend Bennett's funeral. How sad that a relationship that could have been a comfort and blessing in the final years of life ceased to exist altogether. And it could have been kept in tact with an occasional note, phone call, or email.

Recently, I received a phone call from a woman with whom I had been close friends twenty years ago. We had been a part of a small neighborhood group. During our conversation she reflected, "I have never felt as connected to a group of people nor had friends as dear as I did in that group." I realized the same was true for me! As we reminisced about those days, my heart longed for that kind of community. It takes effort, action, and planning to stay connected with friends. But that is the kind of connection God intended for His people.

Here are some simple and practical ways to stay connected to your family and friends — especially those who live far away:

1. *Use the telephone.* Ask your adult children to give you a convenient time to call. I talk to my daughter almost every day, but we set a particular time for me to talk with the grandkids. About once a week, I take time to talk to each one. You know you are calling too often if the grandchildren don't want to talk. It should be a time they look forward to. But for very young children and teenagers, have patience, and don't expect long answers.

Sometimes you have to be creative to make phone calls to your grandchildren worthwhile, depending on their ages. It doesn't work to ask, "How are you?"

or "What are you doing?" Ask specific questions about gymnastics or school projects. Share an experience you've had that will be of interest — like seeing a family of ducks nesting in your front yard. Become students of your grandkids, and know their interests. For example, my nine-year-old Kylee loves cooking. She is always eager to share a new recipe she has cooked for her family.

I like to pray for my grandchildren over the phone. I ask them if they have a special request before I pray. They may feel a little embarrassed the first time you do this, but they will soon grow to love it.

Be consistent in keeping up with friends by telephone. Our busy lives rob us of close connections. Even if we have good intentions, we let daily tasks crowd out the truly important activities like talking on the phone or getting together. Email is so quick and convenient. But it is not as intimate as hearing the voices of those you love. Mark a reminder on your calendar if necessary, and then make that call or get together.

2. *Correspond by email.* Email is a wonderful, quick way to keep in touch — though not as effective as a phone call. But use it. As I have recently experienced, you can connect with long lost relatives and friends through email. You can even email your grandchildren at their parent's email address. This is an easy way to stay in touch. But what do you write?

One thing that our grandkids love is stories. When we are together in a car, they will invariably ask us to tell stories of their parents when they were little, or of our own childhoods. We try to email stories to our grandkids as often as we can. Their mother prints these out and keeps them in a special notebook. It is one way to memorialize your family's history and pass it along. I also write prayers for the children — especially if one of them is sick. My daughter tells me that the kids love this, and ask to have the prayer printed out and put in their notebook.

3. *Correspond by snail mail.* Send cards, letters, and gift packets. Using stamps to mail something is about as obsolete as VCR's and cameras with film. But it does have its advantages, especially in corresponding with your grandkids. They will never appreciate a phone call or email as much as receiving a special envelope or package with their names on it. Send them dollar bills, stickers, or small gifts. Again, if you know the interests of your grandchildren,

you can include some item they will appreciate. If one loves sports, save sports clippings. If one likes horses, collect pictures and articles about horses. I like to occasionally surprise the kids with a care package: small toys, gum, candy, puzzles, books, etc. The important thing is to stay connected. Let your children and grandchildren know you want to be part of their lives.

4. *Make the most of personal visits.* For many years, my daughter's family lived a half an hour away. We often had meals together either at our home or at their farm. Every weekend possible, we had one grandchild for an overnight and part of the next day. He or she was queen or king for a day. They got to do anything (within reason) they wanted to do. While we loved being together with the whole family, this visit became his or her special time when we could focus exclusively on one child.

Now that they all live in another state, we try to make our visits, either here or at their home, distinctive. When we have more time, like over the Christmas holidays, we try to complete a project with the grandchildren (like sewing aprons or making bird houses). We have taken short day trips together (like a drive to the mountains). Last Christmas, we drove up to Niagara Falls together. If time is short, go for walks, collect leaves and wildflowers, or visit a museum — activities the kids (and their parents) will remember. If you cannot be with them as much as you'd like, at least try to make your times together memorable and special. It takes planning and effort, but it's worth it.

Connect through Hospitality

Hospitality is a lost art in today's busy world, but opening our homes to others is one of the best ways to stay connected and build close friendships. 1 Peter 4:9 says "… be hospitable to one another without complaining."

A modern definition of "hospitality" is "the practice of welcoming guests or strangers with warmth and generosity." The original word *hospes* means a guest or host. From this word come the names of institutions such as hospitals, hospices, inns, and hotels.[6]

Hospitality is not the same as taking friends out to dinner. Hospitality is definitely linked with having guests in your home — whether your home is a studio apartment or a mansion.

Hospitality is not only a directive for the church, it's a privilege and can be one of the most rewarding rituals of Christian fellowship. Anyone can be hospitable. Our Christian homes are powerful tools to reach out — not just to our faith community but to a hurting world.

One of the greatest joys Jerry and I experienced as a newly married couple was inviting recovering alcoholics from a rehab center over to our small home for Sunday dinner. Most of them had long since destroyed all family relationships and were completely alone. Cecil was one of the men who joined us many times. We would talk and laugh and relax together for hours. Our home environment, which we completely took for granted, was a huge treat for Cecil and the others who knew only the cold, unwelcoming surroundings of an institution. These were men who could never return the favor, making it the *best*, most rewarding form of hospitality.

Perhaps the idea of having people in your home is frightening or intimidating. You may not feel you are gifted in that area, or you may feel your home is too small or shabby. Truly, there are times when it's just not possible. However, you need to understand that the whole idea behind hospitality is making someone feel special. You don't have to have a large, fancy home or be a great cook. You do have to have a desire to serve others and include hospitality in your schedule. You have to *be deliberate* about having guests in your home.

Start with the basics like inviting a couple over after church, or opening your home for a Bible study. At some point, you may be asked to take hospitality to a higher level — having an exchange student or missionary live with you for a time. One of the most rewarding times for my family was hosting a young man from Japan for a semester. He was a delight, and it was a great experience for all of us.

On the other hand, we once had a college intern stay in our home for the summer, and it was a horrible experience. The young man was lazy, messy, inconsiderate, and got involved in a questionable relationship with a woman at the church. Even worse, his departure date kept getting set back again and again until he had thoroughly worn out his welcome. We cannot always expect everything to go smoothly. But it's still important to be willing. You may come to the point where *radical* hospitality is called for.

You may need to take in an aging parent or a destitute friend. If you have practiced hospitality regularly, it will be easier to handle these unusual situations. And, the best part is, you have an even greater opportunity to use your home as a place for ministry.

Become a part of a community. You can begin at your church or with your family. Be diligent about maintaining friendships and making new ones. Be willing to reach out and minister to others through hospitality. But whatever it takes, stay connected.

Significant Living is a Community

One of the reasons Jerry and I feel so strongly about the Significant Living organization is because it encourages and gives opportunities for connection and community. An organization cannot replace a small group of five to ten people who make up your intimate community. But a faith-based movement such as Significant Living gives people a sense of belonging — being a part of something bigger than themselves. It can provide Christian fellowship, an opportunity for meaningful, service-oriented travel, and an opportunity to accomplish more for the Kingdom than they ever could in isolation.[7]

SL offers the opportunity to learn from one another, to travel together to accomplish God's work in other places, to meet together for conferences and concerts, and to take vacations together. Its members can stay connected through interactive television programs, publications, and the Internet. Consider becoming a part of the SL organization.

Connection is all about growing together, working together, and walking together down the pathway to significance. So … don't go it alone.

Action Steps to Stay Connected:

• *Understand that connection and community are better than independence, and they are God's answer to loneliness, fatigue, fear and intimidation, failure, defeat, and despair.*

• *Seek out a small community of believers, five to ten, with whom you can form close, intimate friendships.*

• *Be proactive about connecting with children, grandchildren, other relatives, and friends.*

• *Keep in touch through the telephone, email, and snail mail.*

• *Connect through hospitality. Take action to start with the basics, then take hospitality to a higher level.*

• *Consider becoming a part of a faith-based organization like Significant Living.*

Suggested Reading

Loving Your Relatives, Even When You Don't See Eye to Eye, David and Claudia Arp & John and Margaret Bell

Parenting Your Adult Child, Ross Campbell and Gary Chapman

Once a Parent, Always a Parent, Stephen A. Bly

Grace Awakening, Charles Swindoll

No Time for Sex, David and Claudia Arp

Girlfriend Gatherings, Janet Holm McHenry

Realities of Aging

I started with nothing – I still have most of it.

Seen it all – done it all – can't remember most of it.

In dog years – I'm dead.

The best way to forget all your troubles is to wear tight shoes.

My mind not only wonders - sometimes it leaves completely.

I know what Victoria's Secret is. Nobody over 30 can fit into their stuff.

Time may be a great healer, but it's a lousy beautician.

Brain cells come and go, but fat cells live forever.

*I started going bald very early. In fact, in high school
I was voted "Most Likely to Recede."*

*I don't feel 80. In fact, I don't feel anything until noon.
Then it's time for my nap. (Bob Hope)*

*I am an old man and have known a great many troubles,
but most of them never happened. (Mark Twain)*

*When I get up in the morning, the first thing I do
is read the obituaries. If my name's not there, I shave. (George Burns)*

*By all means, go ahead and mellow with age.
Just be careful not to get rotten.*

By the time a man finds greener pastures, he's too old to climb the fence.

*Everything Mother Nature gave you, Father Time
is taking away. (Milton Berle)*

One way to improve your memory is to lend people money.

*He's reached the age where they only put 4 or 5 candles
on his birthday cake. One for each tooth.*

*The real reason old men date young women is they
need someone who can drive at night.*

*I was always taught to respect my elders.
It's just getting harder and harder to find one.*

Retirement means twice as much husband on half as much money.

*There is a time to be born and a time to die,
and never enough time in between.*

Seventh Coordinate:
Perseverance
Navigating the Roadblocks of Aging

Therefore we do not lose heart. Though outwardly we are wasting away, yet inwardly we are being renewed day by day. For our light and momentary troubles are achieving for us an eternal glory that far outweighs them all. So we fix our eyes not on what is seen, but on what is unseen. For what is seen is temporary, but what is unseen is eternal.

2 Corinthians 4:16-18 (NIV)

Our younger son Trevor and I went to Israel and camped out in the Negev Desert — that barren wasteland of Biblical fame. The scenery was astonishing, and the variety of sights defied description. On the mountaintops, we looked for miles in all directions, drinking in breathtaking vistas. We stood on the edge of the ancient Sinai Desert where God gave Moses the Ten Commandments. Under the blazing Israeli sun, we climbed steep, ragged peaks, often hanging on by our fingers over the abyss — terrified to go on, yet knowing that we could not stop!

We couldn't stop because those mountaintops, despite their fantastic beauty, were, for all practical purposes, dead. Oh, sure, there was some scruffy vegetation — a thorny shrub here and a brownish patch of withered grass there. But nothing to eat. Nothing to drink. Nothing to sustain life.

As exhilarating as the peak might be, we could not stay on the mountaintop. There was no future for us there. Had we stayed, we would have died of hunger, thirst, and exposure. We had to return to the valley.

In the valleys of the Negev, where we camped with our guide each evening, the sights, sounds, and smells were dramatically different from those on the mountaintop. Sloping deep into the earth, the valleys were wonderfully cool and abundant with life. There were herbs that made superb tea, sweet berries with enormous concentrations of vitamin C, plants used to make powerful medicines, and thick patches of shady eucalyptus. Below the canyon cliffs lay a fresh supply of water where the ibex and other desert animals gathered.

As we left Israel, Trevor and I shared a new level of appreciation for the design of God's earth — and, in fact, the design of our lives. The mountaintops are for thrills, edification, and rejoicing. But sooner or later, you have to learn the life-giving lessons of the valley.

Abraham Lincoln said, "In the end, it's not the years in your life that count, it's the life in your years!" How can we live each moment of our lives to the fullest — in spite of the roadblocks? A big part of getting through our trials is developing the character trait of perseverance.

The Valley – Life or Death?

Perseverance is a critical building block of significance because the aging years *always* bring challenges and changes — the valleys. Though the young also experience trials, second halfers can often encounter a barrage of life's challenges all at the same time. Older, weary travelers can get disillusioned. Rather than having a faith made stronger through the years, they may have shifted to spiritual "cruise control." Some blame God, allowing the trials to shake the very foundation of their faith. The good news: God does not allow us to experience suffering and loss to bring death. He intends for the inevitable valleys to bring life — growth, rejuvenation, and victory.

One important safeguard for navigating the roadblocks of aging is to *expect them.* Don't be surprised by trials. Of course, it is desirable to keep a positive attitude and expect God's blessings and care. But if you somehow think you are exempt from the valleys of life, the impact will be more devastating when they do arrive.

What do some of the roadblocks look like? They can take the form of illness, death of loved ones, disappointment, unwanted change, or caring for elderly parents. Retirement alone can be devastating, especially for men.

We will address some of these common obstacles, but let's begin with a hindrance to significance that plagues many and is perhaps not so obvious. We recognize it as low self-esteem.

Low Self-Esteem

Low self-esteem is one of the greatest barriers to success and significance at any age. If we possess a negative image of ourselves, our effectiveness is hampered, making it difficult to fulfill God's plan for our lives. We may hear from God, and have a vision, but lack the confidence to accomplish our goal. Shirley and I understand firsthand how daunting this obstacle can be.

Shirley grew up in a small blue-collar town on the outskirts of New Orleans. Her neighborhood was called "Tiger Town" to signify it's character: rough, dangerous, and shabby. The town was dominated by the tall smoke stack of the Kaiser Aluminum factory where Shirley's dad worked for more than thirty years.

Though she didn't have a lot of affIrmation, and no Christian home, Shirley had a happy childhood and caring parents. However, she struggled with issues of low self-esteem as a young person. With God's help, Shirley has accomplished much in her life, but, still today, the feelings of inadequacy often nag her.

I, too, struggled with poor self-esteem as a child. My appearance didn't help. My protruding teeth and five years of braces made me extremely self-conscious. Kids in school made fun of me and called me names. As mentioned earlier, I acted out and became a discipline problem to cover my feelings of worthlessness. I struggled for years with a flawed perception of myself.

My dad had self-esteem issues of his own. For many years before my father became a Christian, he looked to alcohol as an escape from his insecurities, inadequacies, and fears. Sadly, the alcohol sent him on a downward spiral that only increased his self-loathing. He was embarrassed by his behavior. Some days he would come home in a drunken stupor and do crazy things. He broke lamps. He shouted into the street. Later, when he sobered up, he would apologize, humiliated.

My dad was a good man caught in the grip of insecurity and Satan's lies. Drinking became a mountain of trash in his life that seemed impossible to remove.

Actually, I wasn't that embarrassed by his drinking. Lots of my friends' fathers drank. The real source of my humiliation was his job: my dad drove a garbage truck. Although sanitation work is good, steady employment, I didn't see it that way. My friends' fathers had more "noble" jobs. Freddy's father was an accountant, and their family had a nice house with all the amenities. For thirty-seven years, my father drove a garbage route. Whenever he came up for promotion to foreman, he declined. He just could not see himself as a manager. Our family was always poor.

But though I didn't realize it at the time, there was much I could be proud of in my dad. He was a good father, a hard worker, and a man of character. I sometimes rode his route with him. I was thrilled to sit in the cab of that massive truck and watch my father in action. He always looked clean and sharp. His hair was always neatly combed, and everyday his khaki pants and white shirt were starched and pressed.

The people who ran the businesses on his route knew him by name and enjoyed it when he stopped to talk. He was welcomed as a favored visitor in their restaurants. Dad did his job well. In fact, he was on such good terms with the head of Dallas Sanitation that he secured me an excellent summer job in the Sanitation office three years in a row. As I sat in the neat offices, far from the menial labor most of my high school buddies were enduring, it dawned on me just how special my father really was. When I was introduced, people would nod, smile, and say, "Oh, you're Rose's kid." He was well-respected by the businessmen on his route, his bosses, and his fellow workers. Dad taught me, without my knowing it, traits like perseverance, dignity, consistency, and hard work — traits I have grown to respect and treasure.

Now that I'm a father and a grandfather myself, I tell myself a different story about my childhood, my father, and me. When our daughter Vanessa was in the third grade, Shirley and I received some distressing news from her school. She and several other children had been teasing and taunting a little girl because of her father's vocation: he was a garbage man. I immediately called the little girl's mother, apologized for my daughter's misbehavior, and assured her that I would take action to correct it. Then I told her that my father had had the same occupation as her husband, and I described his positive example to me as I grew into adulthood.

That afternoon I sat one nervous third-grader on my lap and asked her to tell me about the trouble at school. She related her side of the story; then it was my turn. "Do you know what Grandpa Rose did when I was in third grade like you, and he was a dad like me?" Vanessa fidgeted anxiously. This was a curve ball. She loved her granddad. He could do no wrong. "No," she responded uneasily. "What?"

"He was a garbage man."

Vanessa straightened up; her dark eyes widened. "Really?" she squealed. Well, then, she decided, being a garbage man must be a good thing. She returned to school, went to the little girl, and offered a big, heartfelt apology.

Have you spent the first half of your life struggling with feelings of worthlessness or inadequacy? Do you look back at mistakes, bad choices, or just lack of opportunity and wish your life could have been different?

Perhaps you have lived your life as a confident, successful person and never had a self-esteem problem — until you reached retirement age. Our culture's worship of youth, a forced retirement, or feeling that your useful years are over has given you a flawed self-image for the first time in your life. Don't let that poor self-image cripple your potential for significance. Take steps to build your self esteem. Here are some suggestions:

- *Become familiar with the hundreds of promises in the Bible. Here are a few references to get you started: Psalm 46:1-3; 37:24; 55:22; Job 8:21; Nahum 1:7; Jeremiah 29:11; John 16:33*
- *Read the Psalms everyday.*
- *Deal with past mistakes by asking God's forgiveness; then move on.*
- *Surround yourself with affirming, encouraging friends. Get the negative people out of your life if possible. Don't accept negative messages about yourself.*
- *Focus on your strengths, and submit your weaknesses to God.*
- *Ask God to give you a healthy view of yourself.*
- *Remember that your true value was demonstrated by Christ's death on the cross.*[1]

Disappointment

Shirley

The year was 1920. Standing before the missions examining board was a young man named Oswald Smith. One dream dominated his heart. He wanted to be a missionary. Now at last, his prayer would be answered. When the examination was over, the board turned Oswald Smith down. He did not meet their qualifications. He had set his direction, but now life gave him a detour. What would he do? As Oswald Smith prayed, God planted another idea in his heart. If he could not go abroad as a missionary, he would build a church that would send out missionaries. And that's exactly what he did. Oswald Smith

160

pastored The People's Church in Toronto, Canada, which sent out more missionaries than any other church at that time. Oswald Smith brought God into the situation, and God transformed his detour into a main thoroughfare of service.[2]

Life offers a smorgasbord of joys, sorrows, victories, and disappointments. We all face them. Perseverance carries us through them with our faith intact. When we experience crushing disappointments, we must call on our survival faith, and like Oswald Smith, find ways to turn our detours into pathways of service and blessing. Jerry and I had one such disappointment that God turned into a profound blessing.

I knew something was terribly wrong. My daughter had been crying. As she handed me the folded sheet of paper, her eyes filled again with tears, and she looked down at the floor. Vanessa had always had trouble putting her thoughts into verbal words. She was quiet. She was better at expressing herself on paper.

The letter contained the words any parent of an unmarried teenaged daughter dreads hearing, *"Mom, I'm pregnant."* Vanessa went on to explain how sorry she and Greg were and asked for our support even though she would understand if we never spoke to her again.

I felt like I had been hit in the chest with a two-by-four. I couldn't breathe. I didn't know if I should cry, scream, hug her, or crumple to the floor.

Though in shock, I honestly wasn't surprised this had happened. I knew she and Greg were too close and far too serious for kids aged seventeen and eighteen. Jerry and I had tried to keep them apart, but they always managed to thwart our attempts. They had asked if they could be married as soon as Vanessa graduated high school. We had put off their questions, giving the usual pat answers: "You have plenty of time. You need to focus on getting your educations now," etc., and etc.

The only positive was our feelings for Greg. We had come to love him as our own son. His mom and dad had recently divorced, and his father had moved to another state. Jerry had become a father figure to him. He was a wonderful person, but far too young and ill prepared to be a father.

During my few seconds of stunned silence, Vanessa spoke for the first time. She said, "Mom, we didn't mean for this to happen, but it *has* happened. And if we don't want this baby, she will know. We cannot reject her."

How typical of Vanessa — to be thinking of the baby even now! She had always loved babies. She had no other real ambition except to be a wife and mother. Now she was going to be one.

What could I say to her? As devastated and angry as I was, her wise words about the baby took the fight right out of me. I put my arms around her and assured her that we *would* want this baby, though he or she certainly deserved a better beginning. I asked one very important question, "What are you going to do about God? You are obviously not serving Him."

"We want to make things right with God," she answered. "We've asked God to forgive us. Now, Mom, will you please forgive us?"

At that very moment, Greg was with my husband Jerry, giving him the news. He was in a pitiful state when he arrived at the church where Jerry was speaking. He had not eaten or slept in three days. Now he faced the most difficult task of his life — to tell the man he respected so much just how completely he had let him down.

After the service, Greg somehow made his way to the front of the church. Jerry reached out, put his hand on his shoulder, and said, "Greg, I want you to know you have become like my own son." He couldn't have said anything that would have made Greg feel any worse.

"Could we go somewhere and talk?" Greg asked.

As they drove to the restaurant, Greg could not stand it one more minute. He told Jerry he had done something he had promised he would never do. He had gotten Vanessa pregnant. He had broken his word; he had betrayed Jerry's trust and let him down. He watched as the truth dawned and saw the anger fill Jerry's eyes, and then braced himself for what was to come.

"You're right," said Jerry. "You *have* betrayed my trust. You've disappointed me terribly. But now I have one question: What do you plan to do?"

"Vanessa and I want to be married as soon as possible. We want to provide a Christian home for our child."

"That's just fine," spat Jerry, "but you're not qualified to do anything but flip hamburgers. How do you think you can support a wife and child?"

Jerry will never forget his answer.

"Mr. Rose, you will never have one day of worry about my taking care of my family. I will do whatever I have to do."

The four of us sat and talked for several hours that evening. Jerry and I worked our way through the anger and shattered dreams and plans for our only daughter. We were bitterly disappointed. But the kids had sincerely asked for our forgiveness. What else could we do but give it and move forward? One thing was certain. We would face it together.

Vanessa was right. We had to think of the child. After all, this was our grandchild, an innocent baby who deserved a good start and a good life. However, we were left with one overwhelming question and prayer of our hearts: "God, how should we handle this to bring honor and glory to your name, and not reproach?"

An unmarried, pregnant, teenaged daughter is a challenge for any family. Vanessa's pregnancy was especially difficult for us. Jerry is not only a minister, but a recognized television personality. He had a staff of about a hundred. Many people would be watching to see how we handled this situation.

We were faced with dozens of questions such as: What kind of wedding should we give them? If we had a wedding, how could we pull it off in three weeks? Who should we invite? How should we tell our staff and friends? Would it be appropriate for Vanessa to wear a white wedding dress? How could we demonstrate forgiveness and support to our kids without appearing to minimize or excuse their sin? It was a huge dilemma.

Greg and Vanessa's attitude made it easy to be generous. They asked for nothing but perhaps a quiet ceremony in the pastor's office. It made us want to give them as much as we could without stepping over the line. But where *was* that line?

I was in earnest prayer about this question three nights after we learned of the pregnancy. I had awakened at two o'clock in the morning and immediately went to prayer. "Lord," I agonized, "how do we get through this and please you? We want to give Vanessa and Greg a wedding for many reasons. She is our only daughter. This baby she is carrying should be able to look at her parents' wedding pictures with pride and a sense of normalcy. If they are to be married anyway, can it not be a nice little church wedding?"

Never have I experienced such a sudden and obvious answer to prayer. All at once an idea came from left field (actually, it was directly from Heaven). Vanessa and Greg could write a letter and put it in each wedding invitation. They could explain their situation right up front. That way, no one would feel we had tried to hide anything. But it had to be Vanessa's and Greg's decision. It *did* seem like a possible solution, and I promptly fell asleep.

The next morning the kids' response shocked me. Greg said, "I had already planned to write a letter to my family. But I hadn't thought of sending it with the wedding invitations." Vanessa fully agreed this could be a way to handle things. We all believed it was a solution from God. Following is the letter we drafted together:

Dear Family and Friends,

You may be surprised by this invitation, and it deserves an explanation. We have been going together for over two years and we love each other very much. We had planned to get married in about a year. However, we have decided to move the wedding date to December 17 because we are expecting a baby.

This is very difficult to share with you because you are special to us. We made a serious mistake and we offer no excuses. We have sincerely repented and asked God to forgive us. We have also asked for our parents' forgiveness, and now we ask for yours.

We want to present ourselves before God in marriage so we can have His blessing. This is important for us and for our child.

Our wedding will be a time of joy and celebration — of our lives together, and of God's mercy and grace to all of us. We hope you can share this day with us. If not, we would still ask for your prayers and blessing.

Love, Vanessa and Greg

The letter was exactly what was needed. We expected some negative response, but received only overwhelmingly positive ones. If anyone disapproved, we don't know about it to this day.

It was a small but beautiful wedding, bathed in God's presence — a day of memories to be cherished by Greg, Vanessa, and their children forever. God turned a crushing disappointment into an incredible blessing. Vanessa's pregnancy turned the hearts of two young people back to God. They have been leaders in their church during the twelve years of their marriage and are outstanding parents. God has blessed them spiritually and financially, and has given us five beautiful grandchildren from this union (with a sixth on the way). Greg was true to his promise: he has taken care of his family well.

I realize life's disappointments don't always turn into blessings. But God can be trusted to redeem and restore what has been lost. As Joseph said to his brothers who had sold him into slavery, "You meant it for evil, but God meant it for good." (Genesis 50:20)

Serious Illness

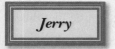

Jerry

Aging Americans are healthier than ever. But none of us are immune to serious illness — especially in the second half of life. I had enjoyed consistent good health since the brain tumor incident. I rarely had a cold and never went to doctors. But, while in my forties, I suspected a digestive problem, so I scheduled a doctor's visit. He didn't find anything wrong, but suggested I have a colonoscopy. I ignored his advice for a long time — or tried to. Why would I take a day off work to have such an invasive test? I felt fine. Still, I could not get the doctor's recommendation out of my mind. *Go have this thing done and get it over with,* I kept telling myself.

Then one morning I heard the startling news: doctor's had discovered cancer in President Ronald Reagan's colon during a routine colonoscopy. Taken aback, I immediately scheduled the procedure. Shirley and I had planned a three-week vacation — a rare interruption from my heavy ministry schedule, but a much needed break. I decided to have the colonoscopy done on the Friday before we left so I wouldn't have to worry about it during the trip.

The results of the test were a complete surprise. "You had two polyps," the doctor said. "One was quite small; the other about the size of a golf ball. I've taken them out, but we'll need to check them." He then advised me to delay the start of our vacation until Monday when the test results would come back. I didn't mind leaving a couple of days later. It gave me more time to clear my desk.

On Monday, the doctor didn't wait for me to call him; he called me. "One of the polyps is malignant," he said evenly. "That means there could be more cancer in your colon. We'll need to schedule you for surgery right away."

I was stunned, and it took a while for me to grasp the truth. But the undeniable fact was: I had cancer.

Within a couple days, I lay on an operating table, waiting for the anesthetic to bring on the oblivion of sleep. I wondered what it would be like to wake up on the other side of surgery. What would the doctors and nurses say? What kind of expressions would their faces bear?

When I woke up, I knew that I was still alive. Heaven could not be like this! I had drainage tubes, catheters, and IV's in every possible location and an NG tube in my nose. To say I was uncomfortable is an understatement. But the surgery was successful; eighteen inches of colon had been removed, and the cancer had not exited the colon. Good news. I was determined to heal quickly. I was not only up walking the next day with a pillow to my abdomen and rolling IV stands, but Shirley says I walked so fast she could hardly keep up.

Best of all, Shirley and I had peace — a supernatural peace. We knew God was in control, and we could feel His presence. It was one of those valleys where we received refreshment, nourishment, and growth.

I was back to my duties at the television station in a few weeks. Other than a very long scar on my abdomen, I had few reminders of my ordeal. I was not prepared for the shock I received three months later when I went in for a re-check.

More cancer was discovered in my colon. Was it a remnant that wasn't taken care of in my first surgery? Was the cancer spreading? Even more frightening, there was a shadow on my liver. If the cancer had spread there, they wouldn't bother to do a second surgery. We wouldn't know for eight days.

Shirley

Those were the longest eight days of our lives. The first two days after getting the news that Jerry's cancer could well be terminal, I was devastated

— filled with anxiety, depressed, distracted. My peace had fled like a fair weather friend. A parade of worst case scenarios marched continuously through my mind. *Jerry is going to die. You will not be able to support yourself and your children. The kids will never be able to go to college.* And on they came, one worse than the other. They were Satan's lies, but I believed every word.

Finally, the Holy Spirit got my attention. I realized I didn't have to be paralyzed by fear. I began to see the lies for what they were — just lies. I began to renounce those negative thoughts and went to the Bible for strength and comfort. God gave me two scriptures I clung to that very long week.

> *Finally, brethren, whatsoever things are true, whatsoever things are honest, whatsoever things are just, whatsoever things are pure, whatsoever things are lovely, whatsoever things are of good report; if there be any virtue and if there be any praise, think on these things.* (Philippians 4:8) *When you go through deep waters and great trouble I will be with you; when you go through rivers of difficulty, you will not drown! When you walk through the fire of oppression, you shall not be burned up — the flames will not consume you. For I am the Lord your God, your Savior ...* (Isaiah 43:2, 3a) (TLB)

When Satan brought a negative thought, I'd resist it and imagine the doctor giving us a *good report.* When worry and fear crept back in, I'd thank God for the time when Jerry would be well and he, the children, and I could be together doing something fun. I would say to Satan, "Yes, we're walking through the fire, but God promised we wouldn't be burned. We are in deep waters now, but *we will not drown.*"

I was doing battle, fighting for my emotional and spiritual survival. I refused to accept the fear because I knew fear is never from God. The spoken Word of God is a powerful weapon against fear and a great faith builder. Reading my Bible and focusing on those two verses in particular helped me regain my peace and victory. It enabled me to help Jerry with his own battles.

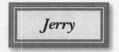

Jerry

The thought of possible terminal cancer was devastating. I had a wife and small children. Why was God allowing this? I wrestled with fear and the feeling that God was finished with me. Every sin I had ever committed, every failure, every weakness paraded through my mind. I wondered if my ministry was over.

Then one night, I felt a strong compulsion to pray. I walked to my bedroom, knelt on the floor, and began to pour out my heart to the Lord. *God, I want to live. I want to raise my family. I want to finish the work you've called me to do. But I do trust you — no matter what.*

I realized I was fighting more than a physical battle. I knew that much of my fear and despair was because I had believed Satan's lies. It was time for spiritual warfare. I directed my thoughts to the enemy. *Satan, you're right. I have made many mistakes. I am inadequate and weak. I have sinned. But that's why Jesus died on the cross. All my sins are forgiven.*

In a single moment, the stifling, black curtain of doubt and fear fell away. For the first time since the diagnosis of cancer, my anxiety was gone. God knew what was going on in my life. I could still trust Him.

We learned the shadow on my liver was merely a piece of colon lying across it. I had a second surgery to remove the additional malignancy, and twenty years later, there has never been a recurrence.

I realize my cancer story might have had a different ending. Christians *do* die of cancer, other illnesses, or accidents. But if God had chosen to take my life in my forties, I believe he would have been there for my family — and for me, whatever I had to endure. I have faced serious illness in the years since, but I am more convinced than ever that our God can be trusted.

Yes, we have unprecedented medical treatments available today, and the aging population is healthier than ever. But if we live long enough, we will experience physical decline. However, God is the great physician. "He forgives all my sins and heals all my diseases." (Psalm 103:3) (NIV) He can still heal today. Let God's Word and the secret place of intimacy with Him give you the perseverance to survive the valleys of illness.

Caring for Aging Parents

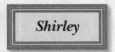

Shirley

My father had Alzheimer's disease for seven years before he passed away. My mother was his only caregiver. It took its toll on her health, but she would not put my dad in a nursing facility. When my mother was diagnosed with cancer several years later, my sister cared for her until my mom passed away.

Today there are 22.4 million aging adults who are being cared for by family members or paid help. That means one in four households has someone at home requiring assistance. The care receivers who are past eighty-five years of age are part of the fastest-growing segment of the population. That means that many of you boomers may be part of what Cheryl Kuba calls the sandwich generation. You could still have children at home and be caring for aging parents in your home, too.[3]

Cheryl's helpful and unique book *Navigating the Journey of Aging Parents* tells us what *care receivers* really want. It is written from the perspective of the elderly. While there have been many books written for caregivers, none have been based on interviews with the dependent. Cheryl emphasizes how important it is to listen to how they really feel, and she gives practical suggestions for discussing tough issues like personal hygiene and even death itself. She discusses the huge challenge of convincing her dad to give up driving.

Cheryl's father started Safeway Driving School in Chicago before World War II. One of his soon-to-become-famous students was Nancy Davis, who later became Mrs. Ronald Reagan. He taught his wife and three children to drive. Driving represented not only his vocation, but his identity. It was a traumatic experience for the whole family when, forty-five years later, her father had to stop driving.[4]

Walking your aging parents through tough transitions like giving up driving, re-locating, or becoming dependent can be one of the most difficult challenges in the second half of life. But there are resources available to help. Talk to their doctors. Talk with your parent or other elderly dependent openly. Listen to what they have to say. Let them be a part of the decision making if possible. And don't try to withhold information.

Sue Black, RN, BSN, says that often when she would walk into a home, the adult children would say something like, "Mother is dying, but don't let her know." And then the patient would tell her, "I'm dying, but don't tell the children."[5] It is so much healthier and more productive if the parties can be open and honest.

Most importantly, if you are the caregiver, take care of yourself first! I recently talked with two adult children from different families whose mothers had died of cancer while caring for their elderly grandmothers. In both cases, these individuals resented the fact that the caregiver had sacrificed her own health to take care of an aging parent. Caring for these dear ones takes patience, unconditional love, and perseverance. But, as one of my guests said, it is a privilege to care for these "fading angels."

Surviving the Challenges of Aging

Jerry and I have shared some of our more difficult experiences with you — not because we have all the answers or because we've handled these difficult times perfectly. But we have learned perseverance through each situation. The valleys have definitely given us life — not death. We know we can expect more to come. Aging, unfortunately, always brings some degree of sorrow and loss.

I talked with a daughter recently whose mother had just had to have an amputation. The mother was struggling to feel normal and go on with life after this devastating loss. Loss and bereavement are hard. Whether we experience the loss of possessions (like my sister and Ronnie), or health, or home, or freedom, or relationships, or particularly of loved ones to death — the pain is intense. It takes spiritual health and great perseverance to move past the roadblocks and continue on the journey to significance. But each time we do, we sink our faith deeper into the bedrock of God's promises, and we become stronger. Here are some simple suggestions to help you build your perseverance.

Learn to Trust

Though we always wonder *why* the suffering comes, we don't have to have a reason, and we probably never will. That assurance is the benefit of trust. When we understand how much God loves us, how much He wants what is best for us, and how perfectly capable He is of changing our circumstances, the *why* becomes less important. Trusting is the first part of surviving life's problems. "Those who trust in the Lord are steady as Mt. Zion, unmoved by any circumstance."(Psalm 125:1) (TLB) "Trust in the Lord with all your heart and lean not on your own understanding; in all your ways acknowledge Him, and He will make your paths straight." (Proverbs 3:5, 6) (NIV)

Ask for Wisdom

Don't ask God *Why;* ask Him *How.* The second part of surviving is to let God show you what to do to get past the roadblock. Here is where dependence on His guidance is a must. James 1:5 tells us that if we lack wisdom, we should ask God and He will freely give it to us. I have asked for wisdom so many times, and God has never failed to answer. I shared a dramatic example of God's wisdom in showing us how to deal with Vanessa's pregnancy in a way that would help our daughter, yet honor God. If you are overwhelmed by your trials and do not know what to do next — ask.

Run Toward the Father

Jerry loves to tell our grandchildren about the time when he was in elementary school and was terrorized by the neighborhood bully. The kid just kept harassing him until Jerry finally had taken all the abuse he could and decided to fight the bully. But Jerry had a strategy. As he left school on his bike, the bully followed him, bumping him off the sidewalk and taunting him. Jerry never looked back, but headed for home with as much speed as possible. As the boys reached his front yard, Jerry jumped off his bike and bravely, but noisily, tore into the other boy despite the bully's larger size. They had a vicious fight for a few minutes. But soon Jerry's father, who was watching from the front window, came out and broke it up. Jerry knew if he could get the fight into his own yard, his dad would take care of him.

When troubles come, take the fight to God's yard. Don't run away from Him. Instead, run toward Him at full speed. How do you do this? Run to Him in prayer. Pour out your doubts, your fears, your pain, and ask for God's help. And run to His Word. The promises of the Bible can be a healing balm to your wounded spirit. They can give you hope and increase your faith. Jerry ran to his father because he knew he loved him and would protect him. You can run to your Heavenly Father. He can put an end to the fight — or give you the strength to see it through. "Let us draw near with a pure heart in full assurance of faith …" (Hebrews 10:22)

Seek Support from Others

In the last chapter on connection, we explored the importance of close relationships. Friendship is most critical when we are going through hard times. Someone has said, "A burden shared is half a burden; a joy shared is twice the joy." Don't be afraid to share your problems (and your joys). If possible, seek out a person who has gone through a similar experience. Someone who has walked the path before you can give you more encouragement and practical help than anyone. Go to a pastor, a counselor, or a godly doctor. The point is — *don't be afraid to ask for help*.

Take advantage of the resources available to you. You can find encouragement and a solution to your problem through a caring faith community. Scripturally sound, inspired teaching, books, or a sympathetic friend may be God's way of getting you through the suffering. "Bear ye one another's burdens, and so fulfill the law of Christ. (Galatians 6:2)

Never lose sight of God's precious promise: "And we know that all things work together for good to them that love God, to them who are the called according to his purpose." (Romans 8:28)

Yes, we can survive the valleys. We can find refreshment and renewal and growth. We may not enjoy them, but we can emerge from the occasional dark tunnels of aging with our faith and confidence intact. God has promised victory, countless joys, adventures, and lots of fun along the way. Keep traveling.

Action Steps to Navigate the Roadblocks:

• *Recognize that our valleys are designed to bring life.*
• *Be honest with yourself about your self-image, and take steps to build your self-esteem.*
• *Learn to trust God in all situations.*
• *Ask God for wisdom — what is the next step?*
• *Run to the Father. Get just as close as possible to God through His Word and prayer.*
• *Seek support and help from others.*

Suggested Reading

Suggested Reading

Navigating the Journey of Aging Parents, Cheryl A. Kuba
When God Doesn't Make Sense, James Dobson
The Thorn in the Flesh, R. T. Kendall
Disappointment with God, Phillip Yancey
It Had to be a Monday, Jill Briscoe
A Bend in the Road, David Jeremiah
So Close, I Can Feel God's Breath, Dr. Beverly Rose
Unmasking Male Depression, Archibald Hart

Laugh Lines

He's so old, his first job was parking covered wagons.

*You know you're getting old when the only thing you do
on the spur of the moment is sneeze.*

I wouldn't say he's old, but his Social Security number is 2.

*He knew he was getting old when he went shopping for a motorcycle –
and the whole store burst out laughing.*

*The secret of longevity is deep breathing — as long as you can
keep it up for eighty to ninety years.*

*You know you're getting old when Medicare will pick up
eighty percent of the cost of your honeymoon.*

*As a person ages, he suspects that nature is plotting
against him for the sake of doctors and dentists.*

My husband is so old, he remembers Eve when she was just a rib.

*You know you're getting old when you're finally able
to resist temptation, but it doesn't come around much anymore.*

Some people age well … for others it's nip and tuck.

*You know you're getting old when the members of the
senior bowling league all seem a little immature.*

*You know you're getting old when your mind is filled
with great things to do, but your body vetoes every one of them.*

*These days, I spend a lot of time thinking about the hereafter.
I go somewhere to get something, and then wonder what I'm here after.*

*You know your're getting old when you figure you can fake it
long enough to remain "computer ignorant" for the rest of your life.*

Eighth Coordinate:
Have Fun!
A Sense of Adventure and a Sense of Humor

Always be full of joy in the Lord; I say it again,
rejoice!...for I can do everything God asks me to
with the help of Christ who gives me the strength and power.

2 Corinthians 4:16-18 (NIV)

Shirley

On December 15, 1985, the Perris Valley Sky Diving Team sponsored a complicated jump. The event featured the oldest father-son sky diving team. The son was Jerry Smith, aged fifty-four, businessman from Wichita. His father, H. T. Smith, was known as "Smitty the Jumper." *Sports Illustrated* once described Smitty as a "retired sign painter, ballroom dancing teacher, and sex symbol." He was eighty-seven at the time of the event — his two hundred and sixteenth jump.

Smitty had already retired from parachute jumping — in fact, he retired three times. The first time was at age thirty-nine. He had been a professional daredevil jumper, but figured he was getting too old for it. Then at sixty-one with all the kids out of the house, he took it up again. At sixty-five he retired again — too old. He took it up again at seventy-three and retired at seventy-six after he took a bad fall that shattered his leg. Definitely too old. But then someone invented a tandem harness that allowed two people to jump together. That made the sport a lot safer. So Smitty took it up again with gusto at the age of eighty-six.[1]

I have to admire that kind of passion and determination in a person of any age. However, it's hard for me to relate to that kind of athleticism. An adventure for me is to find the best department stores, spas, or tea rooms in a new city. However, I *am* all about having fun. After having to discuss some rather "heavy" issues, I've looked forward to writing this chapter.

Contrary to what many believe, the second half of life is definitely a time to focus on having fun! The kids are grown, the work load is hopefully a little lighter, and often there is more disposable income for travel and leisure. Even if finances are limited, a good imagination and a sense of adventure can mean new and exciting experiences.

If you've been putting off trying something a little risky or a little silly, or if there is something you've always wanted to do, now is the time! I heard a story of a prisoner awaiting execution who was granted the usual "last meal" request. He ordered a large portion of mushrooms.

"Why all the mushrooms and nothing else?" inquired the guard.

"Well," replied the prisoner, "I always wanted to try them, but was afraid to eat them before!"

Why not be adventurous? After all, at our age, we don't have to worry about dying young! Why not spend your aging years enjoying life to the fullest?

What does fun have to do with significance? Plenty. We've mentioned that living a balanced life is an important ingredient for physical and emotional health. Yes, a balanced life includes work, giving to others, spiritual discipline, and rest. But it also includes leisure, hobbies, and enjoyable activities.

However, here's a word of caution: It's all too easy to jump from the frying pan into the fire. Many who were diligent, hard workers in their career years jump into their aging years with a vengeance. They volunteer for everything, chase after each opportunity that presents itself, and become more overworked and stressed than ever before. The antidote to the poison of over-commitment is to learn the importance of taking the time to savor each moment, enoy life, and have fun.

You cannot maximize your second half if you don't have a sense of adventure and a sense of humor. If we don't laugh at ourselves, we will probably spend too much time crying for ourselves. "Happy is the person who can laugh at himself. He will never cease to be amused."[2] We don't stop laughing because we grow old; we grow old because we stop laughing. Learning to laugh at yourself, the world, and your problems is one secret to a long and happy life. As a matter of fact, you may not realize just how important laughter is to your health.

A Sense of Humor

When we laugh, natural killer cells which destroy tumors and viruses increase, along with disease-fighting interferon and immune-building T-cells. Laughter also lowers blood pressure and increases oxygen in the blood, which encourages healing. In addition, humor can take your pain away. Norman Cousins, during a bout with serious illness, found that ten minutes of hearty laughter kept him pain free for two hours. Dr. William Fry of Stanford University found that five minutes of intense laughter is the same aerobic equivalent to three minutes on a rowing machine — thus a possible preventative of strokes and heart attacks.[3]

Humor can also help you cope with life's adversities, relate better to others, and enjoy life. It can even bring you romance. Sixty-nine percent of three hundred and fifty brides-to-be said a sense of humor was the quality they most admired in their future husbands.[4] Laughter can elevate your mood, reduce stress, and produce instant relaxation.

By the time a child reaches nursery school, he or she will laugh about three hundred times a day. On average, adults only laugh about seventeen times a day.[5] Can we assume then that we laugh less the older we get? That decrease in humor is a concern for us in the second half of life. We must be intentional about keeping our sense of humor and laughing as often as we possibly can. Charles and Win Arn give four suggestions for developing or keeping a good sense of humor: [6]

1. ***Expose yourself to good humor.*** Read humorous books; watch comedies on TV and at the movies. Take a few minutes a day to read several good jokes.

2. ***Do something silly.*** We lose the carefree abandon of childhood joys to the self-conscious years of adolescence. Some never get it back. Try doing something silly once in a while. If you are too embarrassed to do so in public, try it in front of your spouse. Wear an outrageous outfit, make faces, tease and tickle each other, and make up songs and weird dances. (Does this seem a bit much? I do these things regularly.) Jerry's favorite silly thing to do is to make up really bad puns, but let's not encourage him.

3. ***Laugh out loud whether you feel like it or not.*** Hearing yourself laugh actually causes you to laugh even more. Laughing is more contagious than coughing. One of the games we love to play with our grandkids is to take turns fake laughing. The most convincing laugh wins. And, of course, in a matter of seconds, everyone is in hysterics. I don't know of any other activity that is as therapeutic or as much fun.

4. ***Tell one funny story every day.*** Jokes are so accessible today through the Internet. Write down favorites so you'll remember them. Even if you have to check out a book at the library, find some good stories and practice telling them. They spread like wildfire. While Win Arn was in physical therapy following a stroke, he decided to start each session with a funny

story. He figured the nurses, doctors, and therapists hear so many complaints, it would be a great way to brighten their day. He shared one amusing story about a snake, and, a few days later, another therapist asked him if he'd heard the joke about the snake. He realized many people had enjoyed a moment of humor through that single story.[7]

For some people, depending on personality type, laughter and humor come easily. Others must work at it. Scripture tells us that "a cheerful heart does good like a medicine …" (Proverbs 17:22a) (TLB) It's possible to cultivate a better sense of humor just as it is to cultivate an appreciation for art or music. Laughter and cheerfulness are definitely related to better emotional and physical health, so it's well worth all the fun you'll have making the effort!

Use Humor to Strengthen your Marriage

I believe one of the greatest benefits of a good sense of humor, laughter, and an adventurous spirit is a stronger marriage. And good communication is more important than ever in the aging years. Communication has become more of a challenge for Jerry and me since he has a pretty serious hearing loss.

Not long ago, my husband was in the family room looking through the mail. I stood in the kitchen, trying to decide what to have for dinner. Jerry had been battling a throat infection and was pretty ill for several days. He was just beginning to feel better, and I wanted to make a nice meal for him. I called out, "Hey, Jerry, do you want to have steaks tonight?"

He looked up from the mail with an eager look on his face. "Well," he said, "I think I'm still running a temperature, but let's go for it!"

Well, perhaps some things (like a man's interest in sex) never change. We had a good laugh about *that* miscommunication.

As we age, our marriages go through transition. We might have to get used to spending more time together with our mate as our work outside the home decreases or ends. We may be adjusting to the empty nest. Or we may have to adjust our lifestyle because of physical or even geographical changes. It takes a good sense of humor and a sense of adventure to *enjoy* these changes rather than just *endure* them.

Perhaps the greatest change in the aging marriage is in the area of sex; yet most would agree there is nothing more fun or adventurous than a fulfilling sex life. There is a myth that since older people have wrinkles, drooping breasts, bald heads, and sunken chests, that they are not interested in sex and cannot perform anyway.[8] But research has shown that the quality and quantity of sex need not diminish in the fifties, sixties, or beyond. One of the most reliable studies ever done on the sexuality of older people was conducted by doctors at the City University of New York and investigated the lifestyles of eight hundred people between the ages of sixty and ninety-one. Among other things, the researchers found:

- *Ninety-seven percent like sex;*
- *Seventy-five percent think sex is as good or better than it was when they were young;*
- *Seventy-two percent are satisfied with their sexual experiences; and*
- *Eighty percent think that sex is good for their health.*[9]

We *baby boomers* are staying active and healthy much longer than our parents and grandparents. So why not expect a fulfilling sex life well into our senior years?

Unfortunately, according to many of the women I have surveyed, midlife often brings the end of physical relationship. For some, sex becomes less than satisfying. One woman in her fifties confided to me, "With my body's changes and his, sex at times is a struggle. We never seem to be on the same page at the same time." Perhaps a healthy dose of humor could ease their awkwardness.

Another very honest friend told me that, for a time, her marriage relationship (including sex) declined with age. But things have gotten better. Now, she says, she and her husband are more like roommates. Huh? One lady said her sex life was non-existent. And another said she had never had a good sexual relationship with her husband, so nothing had really changed.

These statements reflect the sad fact that many couples give up on sex far too early. The intimacy and joy of a satisfying sex life are worth considerable effort and attention. A *changing* sex life is an unavoidable facet of the aging marriage, but it can actually be a change for the better — if you keep your sense of humor and don't take yourself too seriously.

As we age, physical and emotional changes can affect our love life: decreasing libido, overall health, stamina, excess weight, stress, lack of confidence, and different priorities. Even when impotency is not a problem, the sex drive does sometimes decline in the aging years. This is when your sense of humor and the desire for fun can save the day (and possibly your marriage).

Because sex changes with age, that doesn't mean the fun, excitement, and satisfaction are not possible. Make sure your husband knows he is still desirable as a lover. And similarly, a husband can reassure his wife that she is still attractive and sexy.

Unfortunately, too many women and men feel inadequate in the area of lovemaking because of their physical appearance. Who can compete with the barrage of sexy billboards or television ads and programs featuring young, perfectly shaped women and buff men running around in their underwear? But remember one important principle. You are the only one who can give intimate, physical contact, and satisfaction to your mate and do so totally guilt free. This makes you the top contender in desirability above every other person or image. The women and men on TV or in magazines are just that — cold images or untouchable fantasies. You, on the other hand, can actually deliver the goods — with love, joy, a clear conscience, and with God's complete blessing. So don't be intimidated by comparing yourself physically to others and holding back sexually.

Frank communication about what both the husband and wife are feeling is key. Think of midlife sex as being much like newlywed sex. In the early days of marriage, you were just getting to know each other. You were inexperienced. You were experimenting and learning as you went along. Chances are you did a lot of laughing together. Well, aging sex is much that way. You may, in a sense, have to start over. But enjoy the process! Aging sex can be a wonderful opportunity to get to know your partner better and to develop a closeness you've never had before.

When sex is no longer possible, the intimacy can be preserved and even improved! Intercourse does not always equal intimacy anyway. That close, soul connection that all of us long for is possible completely outside of sexual contact. It can include meaningful communication like sharing your secret dreams and desires, admitting disappointments, encouraging each other, and philosophizing about life and God. True intimacy can come through these conversations and through any sort of undemanding touch — a back rub or just holding each other.

Bob Moeller, author and marriage counselor, encourages the ninety second hug. Jerry and I have started doing this often, and it's amazing how this extended close contact forces you to slow down, focus on your spouse, and enjoy a full minute and a half of non-sexual bodily contact. It is healing and rejuvenating.

After sharing this idea at a marriage conference, Bob received an email from one of the attendees. The man wrote, "Bob, my wife and I have been practicing the *ninety minute hug.* It was really hard at first, but now we are enjoying it."

Even if you have a very active sex life, intimacy may be missing. Start working now on growing such a close connection with your spouse that when the sex goes away, the joy and fulfillment of your relationship will never miss a beat. And don't forget the laughter!

A Sense of Adventure

Jerry

Shirley mentioned that she is not that adventurous. But many years ago, she joined me in an adventure to "beat the Guadalupe." The Guadalupe is a river in the Texas Hill Country noted for its whitewater rapids. Beating the Guadalupe is something that has fascinated both Hill Country Texans and tourists for years.

Shirley and I were complete novices, but nonetheless, with our life jackets secure, we put our raft in the water, eager to begin our adventure. Our car was parked a few miles downriver, so we had about three hours of beautiful scenery and heart-stopping excitement ahead of us. The first rapids came up quickly. We paddled furiously, trying to keep the raft straight. The roar of the water was deafening — and yet, I was sure I could hear my heart beating!

"The rock! Watch the rock on the left," I shouted to Shirley as we slid sideways, barely missing a boulder. We were racing through the churning whitewater broadside, completely out of control.

Then suddenly it was over; the water was calm. We had made it through the first stretch of rapids. We smiled at each other, proud of ourselves; then we leaned back and relaxed, allowing the gentle current to carry us past some of the most beautiful scenery in the world.

After a few minutes, I heard a roar ahead of us. It was the sound of rushing water, and it sounded worse than what we had just gone through. Shirley sat up straight, staring wide-eyed downriver. In no time, we were in the midst of the turbulence.

Suddenly, in the middle of the spin, I saw a waterfall. It was directly in our path. It looked about twenty feet deep, though it was actually only three feet. (Waterfalls, like problems, often look bigger before you get to them than they do on the other side.) There was nothing we could do. We were about to experience our first trip over a waterfall whether we wanted to or not. I suddenly remembered the tales of daring rafters who had lost their lives on this river. Could this be the spot? We held on tightly as we went over — and under — the falls, filling our raft with crystal-clear, ice-cold water. But the raft was still upright and floating, and we were still in it. This was frightening but exhilarating! And within a few yards, we were back in smooth water, exhausted and happy. We paddled to the river bank and pulled the raft ashore, where Shirley started spreading our picnic lunch.

As I stood looking downriver, God began to reveal a simple but profound spiritual truth to me. The direction of the river flowed past our destination, which was the car. The river was consistent. Its direction was sure. It had flowed through these banks for centuries. We could depend on it to get us where we needed to go. It had some rough spots, some more difficult than others. The river was an adventure. But it also gently flowed past some awesome, truly majestic scenery.

To reach our destination, we would have to submit ourselves to the will of the river. But that meant experiencing all of it, not just the pleasant parts. I could try to get to the car by another route, of course. I could walk, but the woods were full of thick undergrowth, marked by sheer cliffs and other dangers. The chances of getting lost were great. There were bears and bobcats and who knows what other animals lurking in those woods. No … it was much better to accept the will of the river. It would take us to our destination, we wouldn't get lost — and we would experience astonishing adventures along the way.

What a tragedy that so many people, as they age, back off from new adventures when God is just as dependable as ever. The current of His will is absolutely consistent.We can experience more thrills, bear more fruit, and live significantly by plunging in and getting in God's flow. Hear His voice and follow the river!

Adventure — A Risky Business

Shirley

The Guadalupe was a fabulous experience Jerry and I had together. But like many couples, we don't have a lot of hobbies in common. He is very athletic; I'm not. He plays golf; I've tried twice, and we both agreed, without some hard work and a small miracle, it was hopeless. He's a sailor; I'm afraid of the water and can't swim. Jerry is a horse person; I'm not.

He grew up in Texas around quarter horses and rodeos. In Chicago, he wasn't particularly motivated to get back into horses until my daughter, at age eight, decided she wanted to ride. Jerry was thrilled. Vanessa began riding lessons at a nearby stable and took to it like a duck to water. She was a natural equestrian, and it turned out to be a wonderful hobby for both of them.

I, on the other hand, grew up near a large city and was never around horses. I don't like dust, hay, spiders, manure, or much contact with an animal too large to pick up and cuddle. However, it worked out well for Jerry and Vanessa to have this time together without me.

As my daughter grew up and had children of her own, she and her husband bought a small farm and had several horses. My granddaughters also loved them and took riding lessons very early. Jerry was at their farm every Saturday, playing the cowboy.

I finally woke up. I realized if I were going to be an integral part of something my family loved, I needed to learn to ride horses and to be safe around them. So at an appalling age (far past my fiftieth birthday) I began taking horseback riding lessons. To my amazement, I thoroughly enjoyed it. I wasn't the best student, but I progressed slowly and surely, and learned both English and Western techniques.

When I had been riding for about two years, my sweet, gentle gelding decided to start bucking. He had never done it before, but he bucked a few times, telling me he didn't appreciate my discipline. Then I relaxed, thinking his temper tantrum was over. As soon as I loosened my grip, he catapulted me into the air, landing me on my head and shoulder. I sustained some significant and very painful injuries to my shoulder and knee.

After six weeks of physical therapy and several months of recovery, I did, in fact, begin riding again. I needed to prove to myself I could get back in the saddle. But after a while, I realized horseback riding was not something I loved. I decided the enjoyment wasn't worth the risk of riding every week.

I had entered the world of horses for my husband and my grandchildren (and myself, too), and the rewards were many. I can go trail riding with Jerry if I want. I conquered something athletic, which gave me much personal satisfaction and a feeling of accomplishment. And I don't think anything I've ever done brought me closer to my husband.

But I also learned firsthand that when you plunge into an adventure, there are risks. Sometimes we do get hurt, embarrassed, or misunderstood, or we fall flat on our faces in failure. But that doesn't mean we should give in to complacency. This quote says it so well: "Complacency makes people fear the unknown, mistrust the untried, and abhor the new. Like water, complacent people follow the easiest course — downhill. They draw false strength from looking back." (*Bits & Pieces*, May 28, 1992, p.5.)

Don't look back, and don't go downhill. No risk we take is as dangerous as the temptation to sit on the sidelines of life and do nothing. "For God hath not given us the spirit of fear, but of power, and of love, and of a sound mind." (2 Timothy 1:7)

Adrian Rogers tells about the man who bragged that he had cut off the tail of a man-eating lion with his pocket knife. Asked why he hadn't cut off the lion's head, the man replied: "Someone had already done that."

That man sounds a little like me. Though I was proud of myself for learning to ride horses at my age, I've never considered myself courageous. I'm more cautious, especially when it comes to risky sports activities. I have admired my husband's courage and sense of adventure over the years.

I have often thought there should have been two or three of Jerry Rose. Though television and ministry have been his primary callings, he's had dreams of being a Navy chaplain, a race car driver, and a rodeo cowboy. He had a pretty long life list — things he wanted to do in his lifetime — and he's fulfilled many of them.

Jerry has always had a spirit of adventure — willing to try new things and to stay on the edge, both in ministry and in his private life. And his courage is one of his character traits I most admire. He has never been afraid to move out of his comfort zone into new and risky territory. The faith venture of TLN is evidence of that. But his courage is evident in his private life, too. Over the years, he has ridden bulls in college rodeos, done men's barrel racing on his horse, and, as we shared earlier in the book, trained with a Mexican matador and fought bulls in Juarez, Mexico. He has attended a race car driving school and driven a stock car on a Florida race track. He traveled with the Israeli and Christian Lebanese military through Lebanon during the eighties war between Israel and the PLO.

His latest adventure, that he began at age sixty-four, is Cowboy Mounted Shooting. The contestants wear old west clothing, ride fast horses, and shoot balloons placed in various patterns with reproductions of old west six shooters. While not everyone is that edgy, I believe Jerry's spirit of adventure and desire to stretch the boundaries has not only kept him young, but has allowed him to have a big vision for our ministry.

Stepping Into the Sunshine

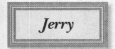

Being willing to experience new things, most of which involve some degree of risk, is key to living a significant and vital life. Living a long life is one thing, but living a long life that has made a difference is far better. We all know people who have lived long, miserable lives. But then there are those who have packed at lot of adventure and meaning into their years. It is the latter who still have a sparkle in their eyes and a smile on their faces.

As for me, I have always wanted to live a life of significance and adventure. I want to experience all I can and stay on the edge. You are vulnerable on the edge, but it is worth the risk because therein lies real success and accomplishment. Years ago, I came across a saying that I have adopted as part of my personal and ministry philosophy. I am not sure who said it, but it works for me. "I would rather stand in the full glare of the sun and be judged, than to find comfort in the safety of the shadows."

There is far too much in life to remain complacent and risk free. God has given me a big vision for our ministry, even though it's full of challenges. Television is changing rapidly, and there is little time to sit in the safety of the shade. There are times when the full glare of the sun is overwhelming and frightening. But it is there where I am most dependent on God and His ability to do what I cannot. My significance goes beyond risk and adventure into faith and trust in God.

I have a long list of things I believe God has called me to achieve in my ministry and career, but I also have a list of things that I want to accomplish personally. My goals may seem trivial and unspiritual, but they are important to me — and I believe they are okay with God.

I have at least three more books to write, get personal life stories on paper for my grandkids, improve my photography, learn Adobe Photoshop, and enter some pictures in photography contests. I want to catch a marlin and drive an open wheel race car. I would like to qualify for the world finals of Cowboy Mounted

Shooting, my newest cowboy sport. I want to lose twenty pounds, eat a healthier diet, and keep a strict work-out schedule at the health club. I can only achieve these things by being willing to stay active and on the edge.

If you don't have a life list, start making one. Then enjoy the immense pleasure it brings to check off the accomplishments, one by one. The important thing is to keep reaching for more in your future and develop (or maintain) a sense of adventure and a sense of humor. We live in a serious world, and our lives in Christ are a serious pursuit — but God has also promised us an abundant life that is full of adventure and even fun. "I am come that they might have life, and that they might have it more abundantly." (John 10:10b)

Significance Requires Courage

Shirley

I recently met a woman who is one of the most courageous women I've known. She is not afraid to seize new prospects and focus on opportunities rather than risk. She is living significantly — with a continuing sense of adventure.

I met Edith Jones a few years ago in Washington, D.C., while doing a series of interviews for *Aspiring Women*. She is an attractive, urbane woman with graying hair and creamy, light brown skin. Her dazzling smile radiates warmth and draws people to her. She exudes class and sophistication despite her humble upbringing in the Smith Projects of New York City.

Edith describes herself as a "wild child" during her growing up years. No one thought she would amount to anything. Many of her friends and acquaintances fulfilled those negative expectations, dropping out of school, becoming pregnant out of wedlock, and going the way of many inner-city kids who lack encouragement and opportunity.

But this "wild child" was different. She says there was something inside that made her reach for more. She made a vow to herself that she would be a virgin when she married, and she kept that vow. Perhaps she had an advantage

188

over some of her peers because of her godly mother. Edith's mother was her role model, though she admits her mother often drove her crazy. Her mother was always taking in people off the streets. There would be people sleeping everywhere. Edith said she would never have a house like that.

However, when she married and had a family of her own, her house was even more chaotic than the one in which she grew up. She had a revolving door to those in need. There was a time when the "family" consisted of eighteen people jammed into her home. She says she was able to pull it off because she never lost her sense of humor.

One day Edith saw on television a news story of a fourteen-year-old being shot. Something gripped her heart as she thought that could be her own child. In fact, she thought, "That *is* my child." She looked for a way she could help get children off the streets and keep them safe.

She landed at World Vision, a disaster and relief organization that had just begun U.S. domestic programs in addition to their work overseas. Edith moved to Washington, D.C., where her job was convincing churches to provide programs to help keep kids off the street. But she met only closed doors and little interest. She was frustrated and depressed and began sharing those feelings with a co-worker. The young woman told her whenever she felt hopeless and powerless that she should just pray, "Lord, have mercy."

One night soon afterward, Edith awoke to a body that wasn't functioning. She knew something was terribly wrong. She remembered the words of her co-worker and began to pray "Lord, have mercy."

Doctors discovered a tumor the size of an orange that was pressing against the left side of her brain. They feared that, after the tumor was removed, Edith would never be able to walk, talk, or have any movement on her right side. However, the Lord did have mercy; she *did* recover and today has almost no after-effects of her illness.

Edith received an even greater miracle. While she spent two and a half months in the hospital, partially paralyzed, she began to have visits from members of the churches she had tried so hard to unite. The people asked her what they could do for her. Although Edith was weak and still in a wheelchair, she knew she must take advantage of this opportunity. Showing remarkable courage, she gathered seven churches together to devise a plan to help the neighborhood children. Within four years, the number had grown to four hundred churches. Edith's physical problem had been the catalyst to motivate churches to make a difference for Washington's young people. (Another example of how God can turn our roadblocks into pathways of service)

When the 9-11 terrorist attack occurred, this amazing woman, well into the second half of life, was asked by World Vision to go to New York to help the victims. She got churches together and distributed money to the needy. They paid mortgages, helped the unemployed, and provided education for the 9-11 orphans. This spunky survivor was back in the same neighborhood where she grew up — making an even greater impact. Now in her sixties, Edith still works tirelessly for worthy causes, especially the safety of our cities' children. God could not have used Edith in such powerful ways if she had not been courageous and kept her sense of adventure.

New Opportunities for Second Halfers

Keith, a dear friend of ours, was quite a weight lifter in his youth and has continued to strength train through the years. In fact, when his son played football, it was Keith who would call his son's teammates and insist they get together every morning to work out. He emphasized to the young men, "Life is a marathon; it's not a sprint." What a great motto for those of us in the second half!

With most of his seven children grown, Keith decided to enter power lifting competition. He explains that, as a young man, he opted out of competition because so many of the contestants were on steroids, and he refused to take them. He figured he didn't have a fair chance against those who took the drugs. But when he hit fifty-five he knew most of the lifters who had taken steroids were no longer around. (Steroids can devastate the heart.)

So he recently began competing in power lifting. His specialty is bench press, and he just won a national championship in bench press for the senior division. Keith will turn sixty this year and is now training for the world, drug-free bench press contest. He has just been asked to accompany The Power Team to the troubled west bank of Israel to perform for the Israeli soldiers — and to give his testimony for Christ. If he hadn't persevered, stayed active, and remained true to his convictions, he wouldn't have had this wonderful ministry opportunity.

In many competitive sports events, there are now senior and disabled categories. Our friend Peter Longo, a life member of the PGA, is a trick shot artist and golf instructor. In learning to do trick shots, Peter experimented with shots like standing on one leg, sitting in a chair, and one-handed drives. He realized that this kind of golf was completely possible and began teaching the disabled and physically challenged to play. Today, he conducts seminars and clinics all over the U.S. and Europe, teaching individuals and professionals how to play golf with arms and/or legs missing or from a wheel chair. Peter has developed a training CD and video, "Challenge Golf," to train golf instructors, along with an accompanying trainer's manual.[10]

Even if you have no interest in sports or competition, there are hundreds of activities you can participate in to have fun. Local park districts and YMCAs offer numerous activities for seniors — everything from day trips to museums, to game nights, to ballroom dancing. Whatever your level of capability, you can enjoy activities geared to your age and mobility. They not only offer fun and exercise, but also a great opportunity to make friends and stay connected with others.

If you are in your seventies, eighties, or beyond, don't assume your adventurous, active days are over. Special provisions are being made to accommodate the disabled, physically challenged, and elderly on every front. And with the graying of America, more opportunities will continue to emerge.

Last year, Jerry and I hosted a tour to the Holy Land. My travel agent made sure to mention that the mobility challenged were welcome and that wheelchairs or scooters could be rented for the entire ten-day tour for a hundred dollars. Tour busses are now configured to accommodate the disabled.

When Jerry and I participated in a Significant Living cruise to Alaska this year, we noticed that wheelchairs, walkers, and other devices of the elderly were everywhere. The cruise ship was equipped with sufficient elevators, ramps, and other special adaptations to serve travelers of all ages and levels of mobility. And, honestly, it appeared that the sixty plussers outnumbered any other age group.

Perhaps you cannot relate to being adventurous. I realize that some of us, because of our personality type, just naturally seek out fun and adventure. Others are more quiet, sedentary, and peace-loving. You cannot change your God-given temperament, but you can determine to focus on having fun and enjoying yourself in the last decades of your life. Get out of your comfort zone. Checking off your life list can be one of the most fulfilling parts of aging. Fun is good for your physical and emotional health.

Just like developing your sense of humor, you can cultivate a more adventurous nature. One way is to try something new and scary once a month. Adventure will look different for each person. It could be signing up for a class at a local college, learning a new sport or hobby, approaching a stranger at church to introduce yourself, or taking a train trip. It could be calling a new acquaintance to set up a lunch date, joining a gym, or getting a makeover. It's not really about what you *do*, it's about how you think — a mindset. Adventure goes hand in hand with courage. And courage is a key ingredient for significance.

Action Steps to Develop a Sense of Humor and a Sense of Adventure:
- *Cultivate a healthy sense of humor by exposing yourself to good humor, acting silly occasionally, laughing out loud, and telling funny stories.*
- *Use humor to strengthen your marriage and accept a changing sex life with flexibility and a positive attitude.*
- *Develop intimacy with your spouse outside of sex.*
- *Create a life list, and work toward checking off the adventures.*
- *Try something new and scary at least once a month.*
- *Ask God to give you more courage to live an adventurous and significant life.*

Suggested Reading

Add Life to your Years, Ted W. Engstrom with Joy P. Gage
Don't Retire, Rewire!, Jeri Sedlar and Mick Miners
Living Somewhere Between Estrogen and Death, Barbara Johnson

If I Had my Life to Live Over

I would have talked less and listened more.

*I would have invited friends over to dinner
even if the carpet was stained and the sofa faded.*

*I would have eaten the popcorn in the "good" living room and worried
much less about the dirt when someone wanted to light a fire in the fireplace.*

I would have taken the time to listen to my grandfather ramble about his youth.

*I would never have insisted the car windows be rolled up
on a summer day because my hair had just been teased and sprayed.*

I would have burned the pink candle sculpted like a rose before it melted in storage.

I would have sat on the lawn with my children and not worried about grass stains.

*I would have cried and laughed less
while watching TV – and more while watching life.*

I would have shared more of the responsibility carried by my husband.

*I would have gone to bed when I was sick instead of pretending
the earth would go into a holding pattern if I weren't there for the day.*

*I would never have bought anything just because
it was practical, wouldn't show soil, or was guaranteed to last a lifetime.*

*Instead of wishing away nine months of pregnancy,
I'd have cherished every moment and realized that the
wonderment growing inside me was the only chance in life
to assist God in a miracle.*

*When my kids kissed me impetuously, I would never have said,
"Later. Now go get washed up for dinner."*

There would have been more "I love yous" and more "I'm sorrys."

*But mostly, given another shot at life, I would seize every minute…
look at it and really see it… live it… and never give it back.*

(Erma Bombeck, Eat Less Cottage Cheese and More Ice Cream, *1979).*

Ninth Coordinate:
Pass It On
Leaving a Legacy
to Those Who Follow

Teach us to number our days and recognize how few they are;
help us to spend them as we should.

Psalm 90:12 (TLB)

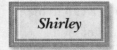

Shirley

As we come to the last and perhaps the most important chapter of this book, I want to share a recent quote by Dr. Billy Graham. Now in his final years, Dr. Graham offers this confession: "All my life I've been taught how to die, but no one ever taught me how to grow old."

His daughter, Ann Graham Lotz, responded, "Well, Daddy, you are now teaching all of us."[1]

Whether we realize it or not, others are watching our lives. We are teaching, mentoring, and passing along truths that life has given us. We have all been the recipients of some kind of legacy, and all of us have something to pass on to others.

My mother and father came to know Christ later in life. When I was growing up, I could attend church only because a family faithfully gave me rides. I knew there weren't many Christians in our extended family. My paternal grandfather was a minister, but he was killed in an auto accident before I was born. I lived in another state and never knew my grandmother well. My father didn't talk much about his parents. I figured it was because they were Christians, and he wasn't. Because God was such a huge part of *my* life, for years I was saddened because I didn't have a strong Christian heritage.

Through a peculiar set of circumstances, I met an elderly minister who had known my grandparents. I explained that I never knew my grandfather and asked if he had any information about him. Reverend Cook promised to check his files, and, to my delight, sent me a large fat envelope two weeks later.

The envelope contained minutes of state conventions where my grandfather had presided as the head of his denomination for the state of Mississippi. It included sermons he had preached and many references to other family members. It was like opening a treasure chest from my past, and I savored every word. However, the most precious document he sent was a yellowed, dog-eared essay entitled "The Testimony of Sister E.C. Rider."

My grandmother's words thrilled and completely captivated me as she told of how she and my grandfather found Christ in 1917. After feeling a call to the ministry, they sold all their possessions and lived by faith. She told of God's miraculous provisions, protection in the face of grave danger, and how they had devoured God's Word, even though the only Bible they owned had a considerable portion missing.

Could it have been my grandparents' prayers that drew me into the Kingdom despite the un-Christian environment of my home? Were their prayers responsible for my mother, father, and uncles coming to Christ — one by one?

Discovering my Christian roots meant more to me than I could have imagined.The unexpected riches of my godly heritage were priceless to me. I realized that part of my history could have been lost so easily. I came to see what a valuable legacy of faith, self-sacrifice, and ministry my grandparents had left to me. I'm inspired to do the same for my grandchildren.

Grandchildren — the Best Part of Aging

When our granddaughter Kylee was very small, her mother told her she had had enough sweets for the day and took her candy away. She was teary and sullen as she dramatically descended the stairs — as though her life had ended. Jerry, amused by her melodrama, asked with feigned compassion, "Kylee, are you okay?"

"Noooo," she whined. But then her eyes took on a clever gleam. She said, "But if I could have a cookie, then I could be happy."

Oh, how well she knew her grandpa. Our grandchildren can delight us, amuse us, make us feel more valued and loved than we ever have; they can also put us in our place. Macey and her Grandpa Jerry once had their horseback riding lessons back-to-back, then went out for lunch. Jerry wanted to encourage his granddaughter. He said, "Macey, you are doing very well with your riding. I am very impressed."

Macey replied without ever missing a beat, "I know, Grandpa, and don't worry. You'll get there too if you just keep working at it."

What will your grandchildren remember most about you? As I just mentioned, I knew only one grandfather and have very few memories of him. However, even though I lived in a different state, I have some vivid memories of my grandmothers. My paternal grandma, Verdie, was fun, a great story-teller, and I remember that she always had peppermint candy in her purse. I especially remember her wooden leg. While her prosthesis frightened all of us kids a bit, it made her unique and interesting. She didn't drive, but even with her wooden leg, she walked miles all over the rural area to visit friends.

My maternal grandmother, with the unusual name of Tiney Ruth, was anything but tiny. One of my fondest memories was her huge, soft bosom and her generous lap — a place of comfort and contentment. I remember her cooking and her hard work. She worked in the kitchen or in her garden from early morning. But every evening would find her sitting in a rocker on her front porch or by her fireplace, welcoming anyone who happened to stop by.

The stereotypical role that my grandparents (and probably yours, too) fit just doesn't exist anymore. Modern grandparents are a different breed. You are likely to see them riding a Harley, running behind a Baby Jogger, or running a Fortune 500 company. You will see them gliding along on their roller blades or working out at the gym. The only time you'll see them in a rocking chair is when they are reading to their grandchild or lacing up their tennis shoes.[2]

Some reasons for this role change are negative societal realities. Divorce, drug abuse, alcoholism, child abuse and neglect, and the high cost of living have often made it necessary for grandparents to step into a "parenting" role. According to the U.S. Department of Commerce statistics a few years ago, five percent of American families consisted of a grandparent raising a grandchild.[3]

Grandparenting is not, in every situation, all fun, doting, and spoiling. You may be struggling to raise one or more grandchildren with limited income, limited energy, and limited living space. As a grandparent, you may have to face tough decisions like whether to take into your home an adult child with grandchildren, whether to lend money to a child for the sake of your grandchildren, or how to relate to step-grandchildren. You may be struggling to remain a part of their lives when divorce has split your family.

On the other hand, you may be gravely disappointed because your aging years have produced no grandchildren. The birth dearth has left many aging couples without them. Why not "adopt" a grandchild? Find a child or two on your block whose grandparents live far away. With the parents' permission, build a relationship with them. Bake cookies together, take them to the park — anything they may be missing from their natural grandparents. Any of us can become a mentor to a younger adult or to a child.

The sharing of values and life lessons across generations is healthy and Biblical. (Titus 2:4, 5) I know one pastor who regularly sends one or more senior couples to be an active part of a young couples' Sunday School class. It has been a very popular practice and benefits both generations. Make a point of building friendships from all age groups. Invite young couples with children into your home. Interact with older people, and learn from them.

Even though grandparenting has changed, our source of strength and wisdom has not changed. We can call on God to help us provide what our grandkids need. A grandparent's home and welcoming arms should be places of safety and peace from whatever upheaval may come into a child's life. Your major role as a grandparent is to love the children unconditionally and teach them about their Heavenly Father's love.

Regardless of what grandparenting situation you find yourself in — whether the grandchildren live in your home or thousands of miles away — you still have an incredible opportunity to pour love, values, wisdom, and attention into the lives of these precious little ones. You can pass along a legacy to all those your life touches — not just biological family. The whole concept of legacy is a critical aspect of living significantly.

What exactly is a legacy? Pastor John Coulombe, pastor of senior adult ministry at the Fullerton, California Evangelical Free Church, says that our legacy is the story of our life. Not only our experiences, but the things that are important to us, our traditions, our faith and values, the wisdom life has taught us. You may not think you have much to offer, but everyone has a life story to pass on.

Think You've Missed the Boat?

A pastor friend of mine, Ken Dignan, told me a story about his grandfather. Patrick Dignan, age twenty-four, lived in the town of Queenstown, Ireland. His sister Bridget had already immigrated to America and lived in Chicago. Bridget wanted Patrick to join her and sent him the price of a ticket. He made plans to sail from Queenstown on April 10, 1912. But the final day to purchase a ticket came and went, and Patrick never received the money from Bridget.

He was sorely disappointed and dejected until four days later. He learned that his intended ship, the Titanic, had sunk on April 14th, taking the lives of fifteen hundred passengers.

Patrick arrived in America later that same year a much wiser young man. He learned that disappointments in life can become blessings, and God works in strange and mysterious ways. Ken often heard his grandfather say, "God's timing is not our timing. When it seems like God is not answering a prayer in the way you thought he should, remember the Titanic."[4]

Perhaps as you look back over your life, you feel you've "missed the boat." You may feel that God has not answered your prayers, and you can't get past your disappointment. You cannot escape the "what ifs …" and "if onlys …" Your past may be littered with missed opportunities, mistakes, things for which you are ashamed, and wasted years. We've already dealt with righting wrongs of the past, asking forgiveness, and getting rid of guilt. But you may be struggling to get past what you *wish* your life had been. You may feel your life is almost over, and it's too late. But it's never too late to start passing along your legacy, and you may have more to pass on than you think. In fact, the lessons you've learned from your mistakes are valuable parts of your story that can help your children and grandchildren.

Pastor John Coulombe suggests several reasons for passing down your life story:[5]

1. *It gives you the opportunity to gain a sense of freedom and completion about yourself. You can take back hurtful words and express regrets for neglected opportunities. You can take away curses and replace them with blessings. That bitter argument you had with your son fifteen years ago still bothers you. You can make it right. You can explain things about your background that caused you to be the way you are and to do the things you did.*

2. *It gives you an opportunity to verbalize your faith and values to the younger generations. Teach your grandchildren godly principles whenever you can. You don't want to overwhelm them with too much information all at once. But when you have quality time together, use it to tell stories and teach them how to live. Turn aging into sage-ing. Be honest about your own mistakes, so that hopefully your offspring won't repeat them.*

3. *Talking about your life is therapeutic and brings healing. Getting things out in the open is the best way to right wrongs of the past — whether you are the guilty party or the victim. That's why I suggested earlier in the book to write letters. Any pastor has heard his share of deathbed confessions. If you have any skeletons in your closet, deal with them now.*

Vehicles for Reviewing Your Life

Leaving our history and legacy to our offspring takes time and work. But it is worth every moment. How I wish I had taken the time to sit and talk with my grandparents — and my parents, for that matter, about the history of our family. When we grow into adulthood, we are usually so busy with our own career and family, we just don't have the time or see the value of exploring family history. And when we finally realize how important that information is, it's often too late. When a person dies, it's like losing a library. Don't let your history be lost.

Following are suggestions that Pastor John gives for capturing your life for those you love.[6] Some of these techniques require skill, but most entail only a desire and a willingness to put forth the effort. Don't think you have to be an expert. It's the thought and meaning behind the effort that count.

1. **Write down your story.** Experiences and memories that seem very commonplace to you may be extraordinary to your offspring. You can do this by writing an autobiography, journaling, or writing letters. It doesn't matter if you aren't a great writer. This is only for your children and grandchildren (and their children). John Thill suggests beginning a ministry of correspondence. Either through letters, email, or the

telephone, encourage others with what you have learned about God, His Word, prayer, God's trustworthiness, and taking risks. Jerry and I knew a Navy chaplain years ago who made a habit of writing at least one letter a day to a family member from wherever he was in the world. In the letters he described what was happening in his life that day. He always kept a copy. It produced an accurate account of his very interesting life with no extra effort.

2. ***Record an oral history on audio or tell your story on video.*** Your life experiences in your own voice will make your story even more precious. Of course, be prepared to transfer this recording as technology changes.

3. ***If you are especially creative, write poetry.*** Be sure to label poems, photographs, paintings, and other memorabilia. Old photographs are of no use to future generations if they don't know who is in the photos.

4. ***Create a family tree, and investigate your genealogy.*** There are Websites and Web services that make this easier than ever.

5. ***Take your kids and grandkids to the place of your childhood.*** Walk them through your birthplace, your old neighborhood and playground, your elementary and high schools, your church, etc. Tell them stories of each place — where you got into trouble, where you were converted, the lessons you learned.

6. ***Give away your stuff.*** Don't wait until you are old to start giving the children and grandchildren your possessions. And don't assume no one will want them. Even items that seem worthless to you may be special to your grandkids. Go through boxes in your attic or basement, and ask the kids what they want. Books, bibles, awards, sermons, old costume jewelry, hats, etc., make treasured gifts. I love Blue Willow china. I used that dish pattern for years until my family was thoroughly tired of it. When I changed my kitchen to green, the dishes got packed away. Neither my daughter nor my daughters-in-law wanted them. But Macey, my eleven-year-old granddaughter, heard me talking about the china. She cried, "I want those dishes, Grandma. I'll put them in my hope chest." Now, whenever she sees the familiar pattern she says, "There's some of my dishes." I wore my original wedding dress at my twenty-fifth anniversary

celebration when Jerry and I renewed our marriage vows. Afterwards, the gown just hung in my closet getting dingier each year. I hated to just throw it away, but who would want it? So I had a skilled seamstress at my church make four bride-doll dresses from my gown. The pattern matches mine exactly — even to the headdress. I gave the dresses to my granddaughters for Christmas, accompanied by a framed photograph of myself in the gown. They were thrilled! Start giving away your collections as gifts. Whether it's expensive art pieces or your beanie baby collection, chances are your gifts will be treasured by your kids or grandkids.

7. ***Teach your grandchildren your family traditions.*** Your children may decide to create their own family traditions, and that's fine. But don't lose the old traditions and rituals. Tell the kids why your family practiced them. Pastor John describes a ritual as "taking something as normal as breathing and turning it into something breathtaking."

One of our family traditions was reading the Christmas story on Christmas Eve night, then praying, and letting the kids open one present each. It was much more conducive to talking about the birth of Christ in the quiet glow of the Christmas tree lights and fireplace, than amidst the chaos of Christmas morning. Last Christmas, our son Jeff, who is an artist, gave Jerry and me a large parchment containing the entire Christmas story from the book of Luke. Jeff had beautifully written the story in calligraphy. He said one of his fondest memories of childhood was his dad reading the story on Christmas Eve. You can be assured that piece of art, now meticulously framed, will become an heirloom.

When you make the effort to pass along the story of your life — your legacy — only heaven will reveal all the lives that will be touched. Start today.

Why Look Back?

I have occasionally caught snatches of conversation that go something like this: "Why does he keep talking about the good old days? Times have changed. He'd better focus more on the future." The words are usually spoken by a young person. You may not think the past is relevant enough to spend so much time and effort documenting and revisiting. But, while we cannot dwell in the past, having a balanced attitude about aging means looking back and looking ahead.

Focus on the Family reported that, in a national survey, seniors identified three things they would do differently if they had life to live over. First, they would take more risks. Second, they would reflect more. Third, they would do more things that make a difference in eternity.

Some counselors and life coaches recommend looking only forward, never looking back at things of the past. In reality, there is a proper balance between looking back and looking ahead, between taking risks and being safe, between handling the demands of our natural life and focusing on the eternal.

Scripture is filled with examples where God instructed us to remember the past. Altars and memorials, *stones of remembrance,* were set up at numerous times and places to remind the Hebrew nation of God's faithfulness and blessing. Communion and baptism were instituted to help us remember and symbolize important spiritual truths.

In one such example, God told Joshua to have the priests step into the Jordan River carrying the Ark of the Covenant. The waters parted revealing dry land so the children of Israel could cross into the Promised Land. Then God told Joshua to have twelve men, one from each tribe, gather a stone from the middle of the Jordan and use the stones to build an altar. He said,

We will use them to build a monument so that in the future, your children will ask, "What is this monument for?" You can tell them, "It is to remind us that the Jordan

River stopped flowing when the Ark of God went across!" (Joshua 4:6-8) (TLB)

In the second half of life it is a worthwhile endeavor to reflect, to look back, to savor the faithfulness of God and His blessings. Then we must balance that with looking ahead. If we rest too much on past achievements, we may never move forward to the new adventures of the future. It's all about balance — looking backward and forward, recognizing the good *and* the difficult realities of aging.

Jesus's Legacy

Shirley

If you are still trying to understand the full scope of legacy, take a look at the birthright Jesus left His disciples (and us) before He went to heaven. He included several different aspects of leaving a legacy.

John 13 through 17 is a meaningful portion of scripture. We see Jesus having a last minute, heart-to-heart talk with His disciples. He knows that in just a few hours He will be crucified, and realizes the whole series of events to come will be devastating and confusing for His faithful followers. He is desperately trying, in these last moments, to prepare them, to comfort them, and to bless them. The first thing He does in Chapter 13 is to wash their feet. He is demonstrating true humility. (The best way to teach the younger generations is by example.) Then, in this intimate time together, He gives them some vitally important instructions, promises them wonderful blessings, and then leaves gifts.

Finally, Jesus prays for them. What an amazing time this must have been for Peter, John, and the others! To see Jesus lifting up His hands toward heaven and addressing God the Father on their behalf. And here's the great news! We were also included in that prayer because Jesus says in John 17:20, "My prayer is not for them alone. I pray also for those who will believe in me through their message (NIV)." Here is Jesus's legacy.

Instructions and Commands

Love One Another

Several times in these few chapters Jesus tells His disciples in no uncertain terms to *love one another*. He knew the incredible responsibility that lay on their shoulders. This handful of Jesus's followers must spread His message to the whole world. He had demonstrated love over and over again, and now He was reminding them once more the importance of continuing in that love.

Do Not Worry or Be Afraid; Believe in God

Jesus knew His disciples needed encouragement and comfort. He reassured them that, if they believed in Him and in God the Father, they didn't have to be afraid. One important example we can set is to put our trust in God whatever life brings. When our children and grandchildren see us face life's trials unafraid, it builds their courage and faith.

Keep My Commands

Jesus has spent three years teaching these men. Now He is commanding them to keep His Words and follow His commands. We need to teach our kids and grandkids how to live by our own example and encourage them to follow the instructions of God's Word.

Promises

A Home in Heaven

Jesus knows His departure will be a shock for the disciples, even though He has tried to prepare them. He reassures them that they will someday be re-united. He promises them a home among many mansions where God lives. Our hope of heaven is one of the most important realities we can pass down.

Answers to Our Prayers

Another amazing promise is found in John 15:7. Jesus tells His disciples (and us) that we can ask whatever we wish, and it will be given to us. But the promise does have a stipulation. The first part of the verse says, "If you remain in me, and my words remain in you, ask whatever you wish…" It's not difficult to understand that Jesus could freely promise to give us whatever we ask for *if* we are staying in close relationship with Him.

The Comforter

Jesus knew His friends needed a comforter and counselor. He promised to send them the Spirit of Truth to live inside them and be with them forever. Have you ever wondered how some people face severe grief and adversity with a calm acceptance and peace? We must learn to tap into that resource the Lord gave us upon His departure from this earth. We access this strength by loving and obeying God. (John 14:15) Ask God to give you the Spirit of Truth, the Comforter, to help in your times of need.

The Gifts

The gifts that Jesus gave to the disciples are a little different from His promises. The unique thing about a gift is that you have to possess it before you can give it away. You cannot give a present that is not yours. Jesus was passing along to them treasures that He himself, the Son of God, possessed. Herein lies the real wealth of what the Lord left to us.

Peace

Jesus says in John 14:27, "Peace I leave with you; my peace I give you …" Jesus had peace! How astonished the disciples must have been to hear that — and they would have been more surprised if they had known what was to come. Their world was filled with turmoil. The Romans were severely oppressing the Jews and now threatened their inner circle. Jesus knew all this and knew that Calvary was imminent, and yet He had peace.

We also live in chaotic times. Our world offers no real security outside of Christ. But in the midst of our world, Jesus has given us the gift of peace. We can pass that gift along — the peace that passes understanding.

Joy

Peace is one thing, but *joy* is another. Jesus not only had peace to give, but He said, "I have told you this so that *my* joy may be in you, and that your joy may be complete." Jesus wanted them to have *complete joy.* I believe Jesus laughed, played, had fun, and was joyful. Even now, at the end of His earthly life, He had joy to give away. It is obvious His joy did not depend on circumstances. If we truly embrace this gift, joy will be the rule in our lives — not the exception. Let your joy spill over to others.

Love

Finally, in John 15:9, Jesus gives the most important gift of all — love. He has already commanded His followers to love one another. But now He gives them the gift to make it possible. He says, "As the Father has loved me, so have I loved you: continue ye in my love." Can Jesus possibly mean that we can possess the same kind of love He and the Father feel for each other? Yes! He not only gives the gift of His love, but also the *ability to* love. Is there someone in your life that you are having trouble loving? Jesus's legacy makes it possible. This is one of the greatest gifts, the most superb inheritance — the very love that Jesus had for His Father. Pass it on!

What an incredible legacy the Lord left to His disciples and to all of us who believe in Him. He showed His followers how to live by example. He instructed them and mentored them throughout His whole ministry. He prayed for them. And then He passed along three incomparable gifts: peace, joy, and love. If life has offered you nothing else of value, these gifts are yours to receive, enjoy, and then pass along to future generations.

What Have You Left Behind?

Take a moment to consider the questions in these two little quizzes. Here's the first one. See how many answers you can get.

- *Name the five wealthiest people in the world.*
- *Name the last five winners of the Academy Award for best actor.*
- *Name five winners of a Grammy Award.*

• *Name five winners of Miss America.*
• *Name five people who have won the Nobel Prize.*

How did you do? Well, the point is, no one remembers the headliners of yesterday.

And these people were the best of the best. Now try the second quiz:

• *List a few teachers who aided your journey through school.*
• *Name three friends who helped you through a difficult time.*
• *Name five people who taught you something worthwhile.*
• *Think of a few people who have made you feel appreciated and special.*
• *Think of five people you enjoy spending time with.*
• *Think of a few heroes who have inspired you.*

That was easier, wasn't it? The people who have made a difference in your life are not those with the most money, awards, prestige, or credentials. They are the ones who have really cared about you. When we give of ourselves to bless others, we will never be forgotten.

Finishing Well

I believe most of us could sum up our dream for the final years of life in these words: "I want to finish well." What exactly does that mean? For me, it means at the end of my life I want to know I've been obedient to God's will to the best of my ability — especially in the second half of life. I want to look back without regrets — knowing that the mistakes I've made have been forgiven by God and set right as much as possible. I want to be remembered — if only by my children and grandchildren — as a godly, caring woman who had her priorities in order and accomplished something for eternity. I want my loved ones to attribute qualities to me such as honesty, generosity, and diligence. I want to leave a legacy of faith and faithfulness. I realize that's a tall order, and I know I still have a way to go. But if I can leave that kind of legacy, I'll know that I have finished well.

We hear a lot about leaving a legacy in regards to money and estate planning.

But what if we called it "biography planning?" In other words, what do you want to be remembered for? What is it about your life that has inspired others? Whatever your age, I suggest you start "biography planning." Write down how you want to be remembered and what phrases others would use to describe your life.

Now the more difficult part: What needs to change? What descriptions would others write that you wish were not true? What do you need to stop doing or start doing? I can immediately think of a couple of personality traits of mine that need to change. If you're serious about this, ask another person to write down some areas that need work. Though we have to be ourselves, it is never too late to conform more to Christ's image for the sake of legacy.

Newsweek recently featured Dr. Billy Graham in a cover story about his present days in retirement. It gave an up-close glimpse into the life of this amazing minister and role model now that his public ministry is over. The article took the reader back to the days of Dr. Graham's active political life and the influence he had on several U.S. presidents. Billy admits to making mistakes and having a few regrets. But it is obvious that the second half of life has brought him more wisdom and a deeper understanding of what truly matters.

His wife Ruth dwells at the center of his world. Each evening they pray together and read the scriptures together — even though Ruth suffers from macular degeneration and her secretary has to print the verses in huge type. At night they read and reminisce and sometimes just gaze at each other. Billy says:

I think about heaven a great deal, I think about the failures in my life in the past, but know that they have been covered by the blood of Christ, and that gives me a great sense of confidence. I have a certainty about eternity that is a wonderful thing, and I thank God for giving me that certainty. I do not fear death ...[7]
Dr. Graham is finishing well.

You don't have to be Billy Graham to leave a valuable legacy and touch others in a profound way. Write your life story. Gather your memories for your children and grandchildren, and make new memories every day you have left on this earth. Love the people God has placed in your life. You won't do it perfectly, but do the best you can. Love them with "open" arms. Don't try to control them;

just be there for them. Then pass along the riches that Jesus Himself passed on to us. That will be enough. That is the essence of significance.

Action Steps to Pass on a Legacy:

- *If you have grandchildren, try to have more interaction and influence in their lives. Make whatever effort is necessary.*
- *Consider "adopting" a child or young adult to mentor.*
- *Look back at your life, and identify what aspects of legacy you have to pass on (hard lessons, faith, values, family traditions, etc.). Start passing them on.*
- *Start writing your life story for your children and their children.*
- *Take your children and grandchildren to visit your childhood home, and take the opportunity to share your legacy.*
- *Start giving your possessions away to your family while you can enjoy it.*
- *Read John 13-17, and become familiar with the legacy Jesus left us.*

Suggested Reading

Lasting Legacy, Yolanda and William Powell

Finishing Well, Bob Bufford

Your Heritage, J. Otis Ledbetter and Kurt Bruner

Family Traditions, J. Otis Ledbetter and Kurt Bruner

Lessons from a Father to a Son, John Ashcroft

The Grandmother Principles, Suzette Haden Elgin

Grandparenting Redefined, Irene M. Endicott

Slow Down

Have you ever watched kids playing on a merry-go-round,
Or listened to the rain lapping on the ground?
Ever followed a butterfly's erratic flight,
Or gazed at the sun into the fading light?
You better slow down — don't dance too fast.
Time is short, the music won't last.
Do you run through each day on the fly?
When you ask, "How are you?" do you hear the reply?
When the day is done do you lie in your bed
With the next hundred chores running through your head?
Ever told your child, "We'll do it tomorrow,"
And in your haste, not see his sorrow?
Ever lost touch? Let a good friendship die,
Just call to say, "Hi?"
You better slow down — don't dance too fast.
Time is short, the music won't last.
When you run so fast to get somewhere,
You miss half the fun of getting there.
When you worry and hurry through your day,
It's like an unopened gift, thrown away.
Life's not a race, take it slower.
Hear the music before the song is over.

A Final Word

As we bring this book to a close, we want to thank God for His blessings to us. We have peace with God; we know Him in a personal way. We have a good marriage and wonderful children and grandchildren. We are comfortable with who we are.

Please don't misunderstand these comments as bragging. God has been incredibly good to us. Being comfortable with aging isn't pride. Contentment comes when you have a sense of significance knowing your life is in God's hands and that you are, to the best of your ability, doing something meaningful with it. We are striving to do that everyday.

Our goal, from the beginning of this book, is that every reader find his or her own personal significance. We cannot tell you what that is, but we want to help you on your journey. We want you to have a positive attitude about aging. Above all, we encourage you to have a personal relationship with Jesus and to grow spiritually as you age. Perhaps we have helped you nail down your vision and God's unique calling for you at this time of your life. We trust that you've planned your strategy and, if you haven't already, that you will take action now. We want you to develop consistency and commitment to excellence. We hope that you are connected in a profound way to the body of believers, family, and friends. And we pray that God will grant you strength and faith to overcome the roadblocks you encounter along the way. And, of course, we want you to have fun! In fact, we hope you had a little fun reading this book. Last, but not least, we encourage you to pass along a legacy to those who follow.

Significance almost always involves giving and touching the lives of others. The measure of significance, then, may well be measured in how much of yourself you are willing to give away. You may be just starting down the road to significance. Or, as you read this book, you may have realized your life has been more significant than you ever imagined. Celebrate that and keep it up!

You may have heard of Jim Elliot, the missionary to Ecuador who was murdered by the Indians he had come to serve. The account of his incredible story has been movingly documented by two films, *Beyond the Gates of Splendor*, and more recently, *The End of the Spear*. Jim made a statement as a teenager that represents amazing insight for one so young. He said, "He is no

fool, who gives what he cannot keep — to gain what he cannot lose."
May we grasp this truth more fully than ever in our aging years.

If we can help you on your journey to significance, or be of service
to you, please contact us.* We hope to hear from you.

Allow us to end with the chorus of a song that our dear friend, Rosalinde
AuCoin, wrote. The words are simple, but the message is profound:

Just be faithful to what God calls you to.
Just be faithful from now to the end.
Just answer to his call, give him your all.
A crown of life you will win.
Just be faithful — be faithful my friend.

With sincere prayers and warm regards,
Jerry and Shirley Rose

* If SL, TLN, or CASA can assist you in any way, or to schedule
Jerry or Shirley for speaking or teaching events, you can contact them at:

shirley@significantliving.org or jerry@significantliving.org

or at the following address:
Total Living Network
2880 Vision Court
Aurora, IL 60506
630-801-3838
www.tln.com

NOTES

Chapter 1

[1] Ken Dychtwald, Ph.D., *Age Wave* (New York: Bantam Books, 1990), 174, 175.

Chapter 2

[1] Dychtwald, 13.

[2] William Strauss and Neil Howe, *Generations* (New York: Quill, 1991), p. 11.

[3] Dychtwald, 15-21.

[4] Dychtwald, 4.

[5] Dychtwald, 5,6.

[6] Charles Arn and Win Arn, *The New Senior* (Monrovia, CA: Institute for   American Church Growth, 2004), 14.

[7] Arn, 15.

[8] Dychtwald, 11, 12.

Chapter 3

[1] Dr. Gene Cohen, *The Mature Mind: The Power of the Aging Brain* (Basic Books).

[2] Dychtwald, 30.

[3] Arn, 47.

Chapter 4

[1] Arn, 66, 67.

[2] Arn, 70.

[3] Contact CASA through www.gocasa.org, or call 888-200-8552.

[4] John Thill, used by permission.

Chapter 5

[1] Bob Sorge, *Secrets of the Secret Place* (Greenwood, MO: Oasis House, 2001), 3, 4.

[2] Erma Bombeck, *A Marriage Made in Heaven*, (Harper Collins: New York 1993), 3.

[3] Bombeck, 12, 3.

[4] Oswald Chambers, *Conformed to His Image*, 1950, 1985, 1996.

[5] Dychtwald, 121.

Chapter 6

[1] Lynn Hybels, *Nice Girls Don't Change the World* (Grand Rapids, MI: Zondervan, 2005), 38, 39.

[2] Total Living Drink by Kylea Health and Energy. See www.kylea.com or call 800-557-5700.

[3] Paul M. Insel and Walton T. Roth, *Core Concepts in Health*, Tenth Edition (William R. Glass, McGraw-Hill, 2006).

[4] Paul M. Insel and Walton T.Roth.

Chapter 7

[1] Dan Betzer as quoted by TLN's *Daily Connecton*, July 8, 2006.

[2] Dychtwald, 102, 103.

[3] Rick Ezell as quoted by Shirley Rose, *The Eve Factor* (Colorado Springs, CO: NavPress, 2006), 83.

[4] Jerry Rose, *Deep Faith for Dark Valleys* (Nashville, TN: Thomas Nelson, 1999).

[5] James M. Freeman, *Manners and Customs of the Bible* (Logos International, 1972), 204.

Chapter 8

[1] Scot Bledsoe, excerpts taken from sermon "Why We Need Others," June 25, 2006.

[2] Dychtwald, 136, 137.

[3] Martin & Diedre Bobgan, *How to Counsel from Scripture* (Moody Press, 1985), 18 (as quoted by sermonillustrations.com).

[4] Scot Bledsoe

[5] George Eliot as quoted in Today in the Word, July, 1989, 28.

[6] Herbert Lockyer, as quoted by Shirley Rose, *A Wise Woman Once Said…*(Gainsville, FL: Bridge-Logos, 2002), 211.

[7] For more information about Significant Living go to www.significantliving.org or call 800-443-0227.

Chapter 9

[1] Shirley Rose, *The Eve Factor* (Colorado Springs, CO: NavPress, 2006), 70.

[2] Brian L. Harbour, *Rising Above the Crowd* (as quoted by sermonillustrations.com.)

[3] Cheryl A. Kuba, *Navigating the Journey of Aging Parents*, (New York, NY: Taylor and Francis Group, 2006), 1.

[4] Cheryl A. Kuba, 78.

[5] Cheryl A. Kuba, 54.

Chapter 10

[1] Dychtwald, 125.

[2] Habib Bourguiba, (as quoted by sermonillustrations.com.)

[3] Arn, 139 140.

[4] Arn, 139-141.

[5] "Science of Laughter" Discovery Health Website, (as quoted by Helpguide.)

[6] Arn, 142-144.

[7] Arn, 138.

[8] Dychtwald, 43, 44.

[9] Dychtwald, 44, 45.

[10] For more information contact: Peter Longo, P.O. Box 51285, Phoenix, AZ 85076, www.peterlongogolfshow.com, or the PGA Foundation at www.pgafoundation.com, 1-800-742-3003.

Chapter 11

[1] Jon Meacham, "Pilgrims Progress," Newsweek, August 14, 2006, 38.

[2] Gracie Malone, *Off My Rocker* (Colorado Springs, CO: NavPress, 2003), p. 18.

[3] Irene M. Endicott, *Grandparenting Redefined* (Lynwood, WA: Aglow Publications, 1992), p. 13.

[4] Reverend Ken Dignan., used by permission.

[5] Pastor John Coulombe, excerpts taken from "Building and Capturing Memories Worth Remembering," used by permission.

[6] Pastor John Coulombe.

[7] Jon Meacham, 43.

About the Authors

About the Authors

Television and ministry have been Jerry Rose's calling and passion for over forty years. Starting his career in college, he has served in nearly every aspect of television while also serving as an ordained minister. He served three years as the president of the National Religious Broadcasters and as a consultant with International Correspondence Institute in Brussels, Belgium. He is an author and public speaker, and is currently the president and CEO of Total Living International, which includes the Total Living Network, Significant Living, CASA, and Stonepath Media. Along with his management responsibilities, Jerry is a television interviewer, teacher, and narrator, and also serves as a regular pulpit minister. One of his greatest joys is spending time with his family, which includes three children, a son-in-law, two daughters-in-law, six grandchildren, and counting. In his spare time, he enjoys photography and competitive horseback riding.

For more than twenty years, Shirley Rose has focused her ministry on helping women. She does this through her television program *Aspiring Women*, her books, and speaking appearances. Shirley serves as co-host and executive producer for *Aspiring Women*, the four-time Emmy nominated woman's show that airs in every state and in over thirty countries overseas. *Aspiring Women* was recently named "Best Television Talk Show" by the National Religious Broadcasters Association. Shirley has authored several books including *The Eve Factor,* and *A Wise Woman Once Said...* Shirley is a member of Advanced Writers and Speakers Association, Women in Christian Media, and the National Academy of Television Arts and Sciences.

She enjoys travel, jewelry making, and gardening, but especially spending time with her grandchildren.